AS-Level

History

Stalin's Russia (1924-53)

There's a lot to learn if you're studying AS-Level History.

Luckily, this book takes you through everything you need to know for Unit 1,
Option D4, with plenty of analysis to help you see why things happened the way
they did. Plus, it's got loads of practice questions to test your knowledge.

It also has a whole section on how to turn what you've learnt into a
top-notch exam answer, to help you prepare for the big day.

And of course, we've done our best to make the whole thing vaguely entertaining for you.

Complete Revision and Practice

Exam Board: Edexcel (Unit 1, Option D4)

Published by CGP

Editors:
David Broadbent, Luke von Kotze

Contributors:
Peter Callaghan, Vanessa Musgrove

Proofreaders:
John Etty, Glenn Rogers

Acknowledgements

With thanks to Alamy for permission to use the images on pages 8, 38
With thanks to Mary Evans Picture Library for permission to use the image on page 14
Page 30: Stalin at the hydro-electric complex at Ryon in the Caucasus Mountains, 1935, reproduction of
the original in 'Soviet Painting', 1939 (colour litho) by Toidze, Irakli Moiseievich (1902-p.1941)
Private Collection/ Archives Charmet/ The Bridgeman Art Library

ISBN: 978 1 84762 675 2

Groovy Website: www.cgpbooks.co.uk

Printed by Elanders Ltd. Newcastle upon Tyne.

Based on the classic CGP style created by Richard Parsons.

Contents

Background Information

These pages give you a little bit of background information to the module. You won't be tested on any of this stuff in the exam, but you'll definitely find it helpful to have some idea of what was going on in Russia before Stalin turned up.

Russia Used to be Ruled by Tsars

1) **Before** the **February 1917 Revolution** (see page 4), **Russia** was **ruled** by a **Tsar**, and the **royal family** were the **Romanovs**.

2) The Tsarist system was an **autocracy** (rule by one person).

3) The Tsar ruled by **decree**. His word was **law**.

4) Tsars claimed to rule by **divine right**, which meant they were only **answerable** to **God**.

5) The Tsar had **ministers** to **help govern** the country. In the countryside, **local nobility enforced** the Tsar's will.

The USSR's Population was very Diverse

Russia was a **multinational** and **multi-religious** state:

1) In the **19th century**, most of Russia's population was Russian, but there were **significant minorities** including: • Ukrainians • Finns • Georgians • Poles 2) The Empire's population was **concentrated** in the **western** part of the country.	1) **Most Russians** were members of the **Russian Orthodox Church**. 2) The Church taught **complete obedience** to the **Tsar**, and that **disloyalty** was a **serious sin**. 3) There were many **Roman Catholics** in **Poland** and **Ukraine**. 4) A large **Muslim** population lived in the **east** of the **Empire**. 5) **Several million Jews** lived in the **west** of **Russia**.

Russia underwent Major Economic Changes between 1881 and 1914

By 1881, unlike other European countries, Russia **hadn't** experienced an **agricultural** or **industrial revolution**.

1) Tsar **Alexander III** (reigned **1881-1894**) and his **successor Nicholas II** (reigned **1894-1917**) tried to **modernise** Russia through **rapid industrialisation**.

2) **Industrialisation strengthened** Russia's **economy**, but it caused **suffering** for the **Russian people**.

3) **Living** and **working conditions** for **peasants** and **workers** were **terrible**. **Wages** were **very low** and **working hours** were **long**. There was also huge **inequality between** the **rich** and the **poor** in Russia.

Opposition Parties began to Grow in this period

1) **Ordinary Russians** became **increasingly unhappy** with the Tsar and as a result **opposition parties flourished**.

2) Some **liberal parties** wanted Tsarist **autocracy** to be **replaced** with a **parliamentary** system like that in Britain.

3) Other parties, such as the **Socialist Revolutionaries** (SRs), were more **radical**. They wanted to **overthrow** the **Tsar** by **force**. They used **terrorism** to **advance** their **political aims**.

4) The **Social Democrats** (SDs) were a **Marxist** party which followed the **political beliefs** of **Karl Marx** (see page 3). The SDs included members who would later **split off** to become the **Bolsheviks** and the **Mensheviks** (see page 3).

5) The Tsars used the **Okhrana** (a secret police force) to **suppress opposition parties**. They **harassed** party members. Many **radicals** were sent into **exile** or even **executed**.

The Socialists were revolting...

Things weren't looking so rosy for Tsar Nicholas II, as many Russians thought life might be better without him. The Tsar wasn't going to go quietly though — he used the Okhrana to deal with any particularly ambitious or dangerous opponents of Tsarism.

An Introduction to Marxism

If you're going to study the USSR then you need a rough idea of Karl Marx's theories. This page will give you a brief outline of what Marx's theories were, why they were so popular and how they influenced Vladimir Lenin. Good times.

Workers were Exploited by their employers

Many Russians were **angry** with their **poor treatment** and with **inequality** in **society**.

1) Up to the **mid nineteenth century**, Russia still had one of the **main** elements of an **old-fashioned feudal society** — the land was worked by **millions** of **serfs** who were **controlled** and **exploited** by their lords (almost like slaves). The **emancipation** (freeing) of the **serfs** in **1861 didn't** solve all the **peasants' problems** — most were still **very poor**, worked land that **wasn't very fertile** and had to **pay high taxes**.

2) In the **19th century**, **capitalists** were very **powerful**. They included factory owners whose aim was to make as much money as possible. This was often done by **exploiting** their workers.

3) Workers often worked **long hours** in **unsafe conditions**, and lived in **squalid housing**.

4) Such poor working and living conditions caused **great unrest**. Marx's theories **appealed** to many **Russians** because they wanted to **overthrow** their **capitalist** leaders and create a more **equal society**.

Marx believed Class Struggle would Abolish Capitalism

Marx believed society had **developed through history** and would continue to **develop** in **future**. He argued that society would pass through **several phases** before people eventually became **equal**.

1) **Class struggle** would lead to the **abolition** of **feudalism**.

2) Industrialisation would cause **workers** to be oppressed. Eventually they'd **rise up** and **overthrow** their **capitalist** masters in a **revolution**.

3) Society would enter a **new phase** — socialism. The state would run everything, and **all social classes** would be **abolished**.

4) Once **classes** were abolished, **society** would **move** into its **final** and **permanent stage** — **communism**.

5) In a communist state **every person** would **work** for the **benefit of all**, so there would be **no need** for a **central government**.

Karl Marx (1818-1883)

Lenin wanted a Revolution

1) **Vladimir Lenin** was a **strong believer** of **Marx's theory** that **society** would **evolve** through **class struggle**.

2) **Lenin** argued that the workers **couldn't** lead the **revolution** against their capitalist masters by **themselves** and that they **needed leadership**.

3) **Lenin** was a **member** of the **Social Democrats**, but he **split** from the party in **1903** because he felt they were **too cautious** to **lead** a revolution. Lenin **formed** his **own party** — the **Bolsheviks**.

4) **Lenin** and the **Bolsheviks** felt that the workers **didn't know** how to create a revolution that would lead to a **socialist society**. **Lenin** and his followers were **determined** to **start** the **revolution themselves** and **then**, once in power, **create** a **socialist society** in Russia.

5) **Another group** which **split** from the **SDs** were the **Mensheviks**. They **preferred** a **less disciplined**, more **democratic form** of **communism** than Lenin, and they were **prepared** to **work** with **other revolutionaries**.

Lenin always aced his exams — he loved Marx...

... oh dear, we never tire of a good old Marx joke. Marx's influence on Lenin is very important because Lenin created the Bolsheviks, who would go on to take control of Russia in a revolution, and rename themselves the Communist Party.

The End of Tsarism

The unpopular Nicholas II was unceremoniously bundled out of power in 1917, and the Provisional Government took over. The Provisional Government tried to hold Russia together, but it was foiled by those meddling Bolsheviks...

Nicholas II Wasn't a Strong Leader

1) **Nicholas II didn't** have a **firm grip** on Russia and he **lacked** the **political skill** to save Tsarism. He was also **heavily influenced** by his **German wife**, Tsarina Alexandra.

2) In **1905** there was a **revolution** which **lasted** for **several months**. Nicholas **only regained control** by making a number of **political concessions**. The **most important** of these was the **creation of a Duma**, or **parliament**.

3) In **1914** Russia entered the **First World War**, but the country's **political** and **economic systems** were **unable** to **cope** with the **strains** of **war**. By **1917** the population was **tired** of **food** and **fuel shortages** in the **cities** and with the **loss** of **so many lives** on the **Eastern Front**.

4) In **February 1917** the **unrest** in Russia led to an **uprising** in **Petrograd**. The **uprising** grew into a **revolution** and **Nicholas** was **forced** to **abdicate** in **March**. This **ended** over **300 years** of **Romanov rule**.

The Provisional Government ruled Russia After the Tsar Abdicated

After the **abdication** of the **Tsar**, some of the members of the Duma formed the **Provisional Government**. It faced the **same problems** that **caused** the **downfall** of the **Tsar**:

1) The **army** was struggling on the **Eastern Front** as **soldiers deserted**.

2) The **people** were **unhappy** because of the **war**. **Food** and **fuel shortages continued**.

3) **Lenin** and the **Bolsheviks** were **determined** to **overthrow** the **government** and **establish** their **own rule**.

In **October 1917** the **Bolsheviks agreed** to **Lenin's proposal** for a **military uprising against** the **government**. The **uprising** was **carefully planned** by **Leon Trotsky** (see page 8) and **successfully carried** out on **24th** and **25th October 1917**.

The Bolsheviks had to Fight to Stay in Power

1) Lenin **immediately** tried to **end** the **war** with **Germany**. The **Treaty of Brest-Litovsk** was **signed** in **March 1918** and it **gave** the **Bolsheviks** some **breathing space** so that they could establish their power.

2) Lenin wanted Russia to be a **one-party state**. In **January 1918** he **dissolved** the **Constituent Assembly**, which had been **elected** in **November 1917** to **produce** a **new system** of **government**.

3) Lenin also **unleashed** the **Red Terror** — a **campaign** of **violence** against the **Bolsheviks' opponents**. The **aristocracy**, the **middle class** and the **Russian Orthodox Church** were **all targeted** by the **new secret police**, the **Cheka**. The **Tsar** and his **family** were **murdered** in **1918**.

4) Between **1918** and **1921** the new **Red Army**, **led** by **Trotsky**, **defeated** the **Bolsheviks' enemies** in the **Civil War**.

> By the time **Lenin** died in **1924** he'd **succeeded** in **establishing Bolshevik control** in Russia.

Practice Questions

Q1 Why were Marx's theories so popular?

Q2 What problems did the Provisional Government face?

Q3 How did Lenin establish control over Russia?

The Bolsheviks were oppressive like the Tsars...

Lenin and the Bolsheviks were a ruthless bunch, but they had learnt from recent Russian history that if you don't suppress your enemies then you risk getting overthrown. Anyway, enough about the Tsars and revolutions — it's time to look at Section One...

Introduction to Section 1

These intro pages are here to help you quickly learn the key dates, important people and historical terms you need to remember from each section. If you've got a good idea of most of this stuff, it'll really help you in the exam.

Here's a **Quick Summary** of **Section One**

This section deals with the **struggle** to **succeed Lenin**, and **how Stalin** eventually **won power**.
Here's what you need to know:

- The **contest** to **succeed Lenin** was not only a **clash** of **personalities** but also a **clash** over **different policies**. The **main arguments** were **over** the **future** of the **New Economic Policy** (NEP).
- The contest involved **Lev Kamenev**, **Gregory Zinoviev** and **Nikolai Bukharin** (see page 7), but eventually it became obvious that the **main contenders** were **Leon Trotsky** (see page 8) and **Joseph Stalin** (see page 9).
- **Stalin's** position as **General Secretary** of the **Communist Party** made him very powerful.
- Stalin defeated his enemies by making a number of **temporary alliances** which **helped** him to **defeat** all his **opponents**.

Learn the **Key Dates** of the **Struggle** for **Power**

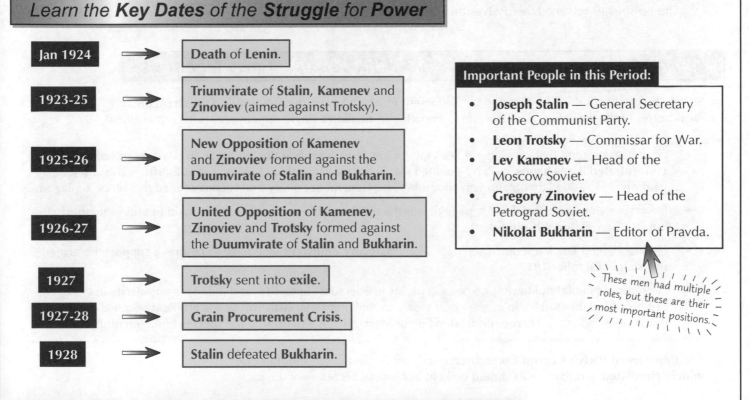

Jan 1924 ⟹	**Death** of **Lenin**.
1923-25 ⟹	**Triumvirate** of **Stalin**, **Kamenev** and **Zinoviev** (aimed against Trotsky).
1925-26 ⟹	**New Opposition** of **Kamenev** and **Zinoviev** formed against the **Duumvirate** of **Stalin** and **Bukharin**.
1926-27 ⟹	**United Opposition** of **Kamenev**, **Zinoviev** and **Trotsky** formed against the **Duumvirate** of **Stalin** and **Bukharin**.
1927 ⟹	**Trotsky** sent into **exile**.
1927-28 ⟹	**Grain Procurement Crisis**.
1928 ⟹	**Stalin** defeated **Bukharin**.

Important People in this Period:

- **Joseph Stalin** — General Secretary of the Communist Party.
- **Leon Trotsky** — Commissar for War.
- **Lev Kamenev** — Head of the Moscow Soviet.
- **Gregory Zinoviev** — Head of the Petrograd Soviet.
- **Nikolai Bukharin** — Editor of Pravda.

These men had multiple roles, but these are their most important positions.

Make sure you know what these **Historical Terms** mean

- **Lenin's Testament** — Document written by Lenin in which he gave his opinions on important party members.
- **New Economic Policy** (NEP) — The economic policy Lenin introduced after the Civil War.
- **Nepmen** — Traders who were made rich by the NEP.
- **Kulaks** — Richer peasants.
- **Collectivisation** — A policy of combining all farms into larger farms where peasants worked together.

- **Permanent Revolution** — Trotsky's policy to secure communism's future by helping communist revolutions outside of the USSR.
- **Socialism in One Country** — Stalin's policy of putting the focus solely on building communism in the USSR, rather than helping it abroad.
- **Grain Procurement Crisis** — A crisis caused by peasants hoarding grain.

Lenin's Legacy

Vladimir Lenin was a difficult act to follow. He had led the Bolsheviks to power in 1917 and he had successfully defended the revolution during the Civil War. But Lenin's death left some tough problems that needed to be solved.

The Bolsheviks had to overcome Many Problems

When the Bolsheviks **seized** power in **October 1917**, they **weren't** in a strong position.

1) The **Socialist Revolutionary Party** was much **bigger** than the Bolsheviks. It was the **most popular** party among the **peasants**, who made up approximately **80%** of the **population**.

2) Most of the **Bolsheviks'** support came from the **proletariat** (industrial working class), but in **1917** Russia's **industry** was **small** and the **proletariat** made up only a **small percentage** of the **population**.

3) The Bolsheviks' **domestic** and **foreign enemies** tried to overthrow them in the **Civil War**.

4) **But** by **1922**, after **years** of war, the Bolsheviks were **victorious**. Russia, Ukraine, Belarus, Georgia, Armenia and Azerbaijan joined to form the **USSR** (Union of Soviet Socialist Republics). The Bolsheviks renamed themselves the **Communist Party**.

The Bolsheviks' influence on Russia

- Russia became a **one-party** state. **All** the other political parties were **abolished**.
- The Bolsheviks used the **Cheka** (secret police) to **suppress** internal opposition.
- The Bolsheviks promoted **atheism** in Russia. Many **churches** were **closed** and **priests** were **imprisoned** or **murdered**.

Lenin's Testament was Critical of All the Leading Party Members

Shortly before Lenin died, he dictated his **Testament** in which he made comments on the **strengths** and **weaknesses** of the **main** figures in the party. Importantly, he **didn't** single out anyone as his **replacement**.

- Lenin was worried that, as General Secretary of the party, **Joseph Stalin** (see page 9) had "**unlimited authority concentrated** in his **hands**" and he **doubted** that Stalin was "**capable** of **using** that **authority** with **sufficient caution**". He added that Stalin was **too rude** to be **General Secretary** and **recommended** that he be **replaced**.

- He argued that **Leon Trotsky** (see page 8) was the **most capable man** amongst the **main figures** in the **party**, but that he was **too self-confident**.

- He highlighted **Lev Kamenev's** (see page 7) and **Gregory Zinoviev's** (see page 7) **failure** to **support** the **armed uprising** in **October 1917**.

- He **praised Nikolai Bukharin** (see page 7) for his **intellectual capability**, and noted his **popularity** in the party. But he added that **Bukharin's** theoretical views **weren't** truly **Marxist**. This was a **problem** because it was believed that a **correct understanding** of **Marxism** was **essential** to the **success** of the **revolution**.

The **Communist Party's Central Committee** voted that the Testament **shouldn't** be **widely circulated** and that Stalin **should** be **kept** as General Secretary of the party.

The Future of the USSR was Uncertain after Lenin's Death

When Lenin died in **1924**, he left **three big questions** that needed to be answered:

- **How** was the **new socialist state** going to **survive** in a **hostile world**?
- **How** was the **country's economy going** to be **organised**?
- **Who** would **replace Lenin** as **leader** of the **Communist Party**?

The **last question** was the **most important**. Lenin **hadn't** chosen one person to **lead** the **party** after him. As a result a **power struggle** developed **between** the **main rivals** to **succeed Lenin**.

The Candidates to Succeed Lenin

Lenin died in January 1924, leaving the USSR with some big questions. The most pressing of these was who would succeed Lenin as the new leader of the Communist Party. There were five leading contenders that you need to know.

There were **Five Main Candidates** to **Succeed** Lenin

Each of the **candidates** to replace Lenin had **strengths** and **weaknesses**.

Lev Kamenev (1883-1936)

Kamenev was the son of a **railway worker**, and he joined the **Bolsheviks** as a **teenager**. In **February 1917** he **returned** to **Petrograd** from **exile** in **Siberia** and became an **important** member of the party.

Strengths
1) Kamenev **led** the **Moscow Soviet** and developed a **secure power base** in the city.
2) He was very **intelligent**.

Weaknesses
1) Kamenev often **disagreed** with **Lenin** on many aspects of **party policy**. This was a **problem** because perceived **loyalty** to Lenin became **increasingly important** after his death.
2) He was **one** of only **two members** of the **Central Committee** to vote **against** an **armed uprising** in **October 1917**.

Gregory Zinoviev (1883-1936)

Zinoviev's parents were **dairy farmers** and, like Kamenev, he joined the **Bolsheviks** at a **young age**. He spent some time with **Lenin** in **Switzerland**, and he **returned** to **Petrograd** in **April 1917**.

Strengths
1) In **1918**, Zinoviev was **appointed** as head of the **Petrograd Soviet**.
2) He was a **close associate** of **Lenin**.

Weaknesses
1) Zinoviev, like Kamenev, had **voted against** the **armed uprising** in **October 1917**.
2) He was **very ambitious** and made **many enemies**.

Nikolai Bukharin (1888-1938)

Unlike some of the other leading contenders, **Bukharin** had **often** travelled **abroad** before 1917. He was with **Trotsky** in **New York** when the **Tsar** was **overthrown** and he **quickly returned** to **Russia**.

Strengths
1) After the **October Revolution**, Bukharin was **appointed** as **editor** of the party newspaper, **Pravda**.
2) **Lenin** once called him the "darling of the party".
3) He was **very popular**, and his easy-to-read **introduction** to **communism** had sold **many copies**.

Weaknesses
1) Bukharin had headed up the first communist **opposition group**, the **Left Communists**, who **criticised Lenin's** decision to make **peace** with **Germany** in **1918**.
2) He **wasn't** a very **shrewd** or **skilful politician**.

Practice Question

Q1 Identify one criticism Lenin had of Kamenev, Zinoviev and Bukharin.

Glossary
internal opposition — opponents to the Bolsheviks inside Russia

There's lots to learn — Kamenev a go if you think you're hard enough...

Lenin's Testament made a lot of leading Communist Party members very uncomfortable, and it's not very surprising that they voted to suppress what Lenin wrote. Kamenev, Zinoviev and Stalin worked together to ensure the Testament was never widely circulated.

The Candidates to Succeed Lenin

Leon Trotsky was one of the favourites to succeed Lenin. Trotsky had organised the October Revolution and led the Red Army to victory in the Civil War. He was the obvious choice as the next leader, but he wasn't very popular.

Leon Trotsky (1879-1940)

Trotsky became a **revolutionary** as a **teenager**, but unlike the other candidates he started out as a **Menshevik**. Trotsky joined the **Bolsheviks** in **1917**, and **Lenin gave** him the **important task** of **organising** the **1917 October Revolution**.

Trotsky's *Leadership* was *Crucial* to the Bolshevik *Victory* in the *Civil War*

1) After the **October Revolution**, Trotsky was made **Commissar for Foreign Affairs**. He **led** the **negotiations** with Germany and agreed to the **Treaty of Brest-Litovsk** in **March 1918**.

2) Trotsky earned some **popularity** for **negotiating peace** with Germany. But he was also **strongly criticised** for **losing vast areas** of the **western** part of the former **Russian Empire** to Germany.

3) When the **Civil War** broke out, Trotsky became **Commissar for War** — he was responsible for the new **Red Army**. He imposed **ruthless discipline** on his troops and made the **Red Army** into an **effective fighting force**.

4) During the war, Trotsky **travelled across** Russia in his **armoured train** to **visit** the **soldiers** on the **front line**. He gave **inspirational speeches** to the troops to **keep up** their **morale**.

From left to right — Trotsky, Lenin and Kamenev in 1920.

Trotsky's *Support* was *Limited*

The Peasants
- Trotsky was **unpopular** with the **peasants** because he had **organised** the **grain requisition squads** during the **Civil War**.
- The squads used **force** to **seize grain** from farms to **feed** the **army**.

The Proletariat
- Trotsky was **intelligent** and **cultured**, but this **didn't impress** the **proletariat**.
- The **proletariat** favoured leaders like **Stalin**, who was **modest** and had a **humble background**.

The Red Army
- Trotsky's **main support** came from the **Red Army**.
- He had **created** the **Red Army** and **led** it to **victory**. This meant he was **very popular** with the **officers** and **soldiers**.

The Communist Party
- Trotsky only **joined** the **Bolsheviks** in **1917**. Many party members believed that because of his **background** as a **Menshevik** he **wasn't devoted** to the **party** and its **policies**.
- He was **popular** with **young** and **radical** members of the party.
- He **wasn't** a **politician** by **instinct**. He **never** tried to gain **loyal supporters** in the **party**.
- Party members **feared** Trotsky would **use** his **popularity** with the **Red Army** to set himself up as a **military dictator**, as **Napoleon Bonaparte** had done **after** the **French Revolution**.

Russia had a long history of anti-Semitism — Trotsky's Jewish background made him unpopular.

The Candidates to Succeed Lenin

Joseph Stalin didn't have the star quality of his main rival, Trotsky, but he knew how to win friends and influence people.

Joseph Stalin (1879-1953)

Stalin was born in **Georgia**. His **father** was a **bootmaker** and his **mother** was a **washerwoman**. Stalin was in **exile** in **Siberia** when the **February Revolution** broke out, but he **quickly** returned to **Petrograd**. He played a **minor role** in the **October Revolution**, but his **Georgian origins** helped him to become the **Commissar for Nationalities** in **1917**.

Stalin *Gradually* increased his *Personal Power*

Stalin **wasn't** an **important** figure in the **Civil War**, but he **helped** to **defend Georgia** against the Red Army's enemies. However, in **1922** Stalin rose to prominence when he was appointed **General Secretary** of the **Communist Party**. Stalin used his position to **increase** his **personal power** and **influence**.

- As General Secretary, Stalin had **complete control** over the **inner workings** of the **Communist Party**.
- He used his position to **promote** his **supporters** and **remove** or **sideline** his **opponents**.
- He had access to **secret files** on **party members** that he **received** from the **Cheka**.
- He also used the **Lenin Enrolment** to create a **large group** of **supporters** in the party.

The use of power to promote allies to key positions is called 'patronage'.

Lenin Enrolment

1) The party decided to **honour Lenin** by **increasing party membership**, **especially** among the **proletariat**.
2) Party membership **nearly doubled** between **1922** and **1925**. The party **changed** from being **dominated** by **intellectuals** into a party **mostly** made up of **peasants** and the **proletariat**.
3) **Most** new members **weren't** interested in **politics**. They joined to **improve** their **personal prospects** and **gain promotions** at work.
4) These new members were **grateful** to **Stalin**, who **supervised** the Lenin Enrolment, and they became his **loyal supporters**.

Stalin had the *Common Touch*

1) Unlike most leaders in the party, **Stalin** had **risen** from very **humble origins**.
2) Many of the **new members** of the party, brought in by the **Lenin Enrolment**, had more in common with the **down-to-earth Stalin** than the more **intellectual** and **cultured** leaders like **Trotsky** and **Bukharin**.
3) However, Stalin's **personality** got him into **trouble**. He was **very rude** to **Lenin's** wife, **Krupskaya**, and Lenin wanted to **remove** Stalin from his position as **General Secretary**, but he **didn't** achieve this before he **died**.

Stalin *Promoted* the *Cult* of *Lenin*

After **Lenin's death**, Stalin portrayed the former leader as a **god-like** figure and himself as Lenin's **natural successor**.

1) At **Lenin's funeral**, **Stalin** gave a **speech** in which he **promised** to **preserve** Lenin's **work** and **reputation**.
2) **Trotsky wasn't present** at Lenin's funeral. When Lenin died, Trotsky was in **Georgia** recovering from an **illness**. He **wanted** to **return** to **Moscow** for the **funeral**, but Stalin told him he **couldn't** return in time. **Later**, Trotsky claimed that **Stalin** had **deliberately** given him the **wrong date** to **stop** him from going.
3) Trotsky's **absence** from the **funeral** made it look like he was **snubbing** his former leader.
4) **Lenin's body** was embalmed and put on **display** in a **mausoleum** in **Moscow's Red Square**.
5) **Stalin** also **glorified** Lenin's memory by writing **'Foundations of Leninism'** in **1924** and he **lectured** on **Lenin** at **Moscow University**.

Petrograd was renamed Leningrad.

Stalin knew how to use his power effectively...

Stalin had a tighter grip on the Communist Party than his rivals realised, and it was decisive in deciding who would succeed Lenin. Stalin's control of the party meant that he could fill key posts with his own supporters and remove those who disagreed with him.

The Big Debate — the USSR's Future

The debate about the future of the USSR's economy threatened to tear the Communist Party apart. The argument centred on whether the USSR should keep the New Economic Policy or drop it like a hot potato covered in spikes.

The **New Economic Policy** helped the **USSR's Economy** to **Recover**

The New Economic Policy (**NEP**) was introduced in **1921**. The **economy** was in **ruins**, **industry** had virtually **collapsed**, and there was widespread **famine** throughout the country. Lenin decided to bring back **some capitalist methods** to **save** the **economy** from **total disaster**.

The Main Features of the NEP

1) **Small** privately owned industry and **private trading** were **permitted**.
2) **Heavy industry**, **transport** and **banks remained** under **state control**.
3) **Grain requisitioning** was **replaced** with a **small tax**.
4) **Peasants** were allowed to sell their **surplus** food for a **profit**.

The NEP led to a **dramatic improvement** in the country's economy. **Food shortages** were **eliminated** and **industry** began to **grow** again. By **1928** the **USSR's economy** had **recovered** to about where it was in **1914**. **Lenin** thought of the **NEP** as only a **temporary measure**, but he **didn't** say **how long** it should **last**.

The **NEP** created **Big Divisions** in the party

Many Communist Party members **didn't** like the **NEP** because it seemed **too much** like **capitalism**, but there was **no agreement** on **how** to **replace** it. The party **split** into **two sides** — one side lined up behind **Bukharin** and the other behind **Trotsky**.

Bukharin wanted to **Keep** the **NEP**

- **Bukharin** and his supporters felt the **NEP** should **continue** for a while because it was **providing food** for the **cities** and **work** for the **proletariat**.
- Bukharin told the **peasants** to **enrich themselves** and **buy goods** to **promote** the USSR's **industry**.
- He believed that there should be a **smychka** (an alliance) between **peasants** and **workers** — he **didn't** want to create **differences** between them.

Trotsky wanted to **Abolish** the **NEP**

- **Trotsky** and his supporters **resented** the fact that, because of the NEP, **much** of the USSR's **industry wasn't** under the direct **control** of the government.
- They also **hated** the Nepmen — traders who made **large profits** from the **NEP**.
- Trotsky felt that communism **hadn't** truly spread to the **countryside**, and he wanted to end the **inequality** between **poor peasants** and the **kulaks** (richer peasants).
- He wanted to **abolish private farms** and **introduce collective farming** (where the peasants **farmed together** on **shared land**). Any **profits** made by the **collective farms** would be used to **develop** the USSR's **industry**.

Stalin **didn't** get **involved** in the debate on the NEP. This was a **clever** move by Stalin because it meant that he could win **support** both from those who'd **backed Bukharin** (known as 'right communists') and those who'd **backed Trotsky** (known as 'left communists').

The Big Debate — the USSR's Future

Choosing a new leader for the Communist Party wasn't just about picking the best man for the job. It was also about picking which leader had the best vision for the future of the USSR. Trotsky and Stalin had quite different ideas.

Trotsky and Stalin **Clashed** over **How** the USSR should be **Governed**

1) Trotsky criticised the **growing bureaucracy** in the party — he argued that party bureaucrats were making decisions **without** any **input** from **ordinary party members** and that the party was **losing touch** with the **proletariat**.

2) Trotsky felt that the best way to **challenge** the **party** bureaucracy was to have **greater democracy** within the **party**. This meant that he wanted more **open debate** within the party and for **ordinary party members** to **not** be **afraid** to give their **opinions**.

3) Trotsky's **criticism** of the **party bureaucracy** was **unpopular** with other party members because they had **benefited** from this system by **gaining power** and **prestige**.

4) The government **Stalin** was creating was to be **totally dominated** by the **Communist Party**. Such a government **wouldn't consult** the **people** and its **aim** would be to **dominate** Russian society **as soon as possible**.

5) As the **General Secretary**, this type of government would give Stalin **great power**.

Olga always wanted to dominate the party.

Trotsky wanted to *Export Communism*

In **1924**, the **USSR** was the **only communist state** in the **world** and it was **surrounded** by **enemies**. **Trotsky** and **Stalin** came up with **different ideas** about how to **protect communism** and the **USSR**.

Permanent Revolution

Permanent Revolution is also referred to as 'World Revolution'.

- Trotsky wanted **Permanent Revolution**, because he believed that unless **communism** spread beyond the USSR it **wouldn't survive**.

- He believed that the **revolution** in Russia was the **first step** towards a **worldwide revolution** of the **proletariat**.

- He argued that the government had a **duty** to **export communism** to other countries, **especially** in **western Europe**.

Socialism in One Country

- Stalin, backed by Bukharin, argued for **Socialism in One Country**.

- There had been **failed communist uprisings** in **Germany** and **Hungary** after the war. Stalin **didn't** think that **other revolutions** would be **successful**.

- He wanted to **concentrate** on **building** a **socialist state**. This meant **focusing** resources on development at **home** and **not** on promoting revolutions **abroad**.

Stalin's policy was **more popular** with the people. Since **1905**, people in Russia had experienced major **political unrest**, **famine** and **war**. The people wanted **peace**, and Stalin's policy also **appealed** to their **national pride**.

Practice Questions

Q1 Why did many Communist Party members instinctively dislike the NEP?

Q2 Describe the policy of Socialism in One Country.

Q3 Imagine you are Trotsky. Write a paragraph explaining to Communist Party members why your policy of Permanent Revolution is better than Stalin's policy of Socialism in One Country.

Exam Question

Q1 To what extent was the Communist Party ideologically divided in the period 1924 to 1928? [30 Marks]

Communists — they're always arguing about something...

When Lenin died, he hadn't outlined his ideas on what policies the party should follow in the future. This meant that the main contenders in the struggle to succeed Lenin squabbled over what direction to take the USSR in. The party began to split apart.

Stalin's Victory (1924-1928)

Stalin was an excellent political tactician. He followed a clever strategy of making alliances with his rivals in order to isolate his other opponents. This meant it was easier to pick off his enemies.

The **Leadership Struggle** was **Complicated**

Stalin's rise to **power** can be **confusing**, but it's best explained in **four stages**.

Stage One — The **Triumvirate** against **Trotsky**

In **1923**, **Stalin** made an **alliance** with **Kamenev** and **Zinoviev** to form a **Triumvirate** (a union of three people). They agreed to **work together** to **defeat Trotsky**. **Trotsky** and his **followers** were known as the **Left Opposition**.

1) **Zinoviev** and **Kamenev convinced** the party to **not** publish **Lenin's Testament** and to **not** follow Lenin's suggestion of removing **Stalin** as **General Secretary**. This meant that Stalin could use his **role** to fill **key positions** in the **party** with **his supporters** and to **remove Trotsky's supporters**.

2) The Triumvirate **promoted** the **Cult of Lenin** and **claimed** that **Trotsky** was **disloyal** to **Lenin** (which seemed to be true when Trotsky missed Lenin's funeral). They also **attacked** Trotsky's **late conversion** to Bolshevism.

3) Trotsky was **angered** by these criticisms and he **published** the **'Lessons of October'** in **1924**. It **attacked Kamenev** and **Zinoviev** for **voting against** an **armed uprising** in October 1917.

4) The **Triumvirate** used the **ban** on **party factions**, which **Lenin introduced** in **1921**, to **silence** the **Left Opposition** at the **1924 Party Congress**. The ban **prevented criticism** of the **party's leadership** and the **formation** of **opposition groups** within the **party**.

5) Trotsky was **forced** to **resign** as **Commissar for War**, which **robbed** him of much of his **support**.

Stage Two — The **Duumvirate** against the **New Opposition**

By **1925**, Stalin felt that the Triumvirate had **achieved** its **aim**. It had **succeeded** in **undermining Trotsky**, and Stalin decided to form a **Duumvirate** (a union of two people) with **Bukharin**. **Kamenev** and **Zinoviev** realised that **Stalin** was now their **biggest** threat — they **teamed up** to form the **New Opposition**. Their policies were **close** to **Trotsky's**.

1) **Kamenev** and **Zinoviev** argued for **Permanent Revolution** and an **end** to the **NEP** at the **1925 Party Congress**.

2) Stalin **filled** the **Congress** with his **supporters** and the **New Opposition** was **defeated** in a **vote**.

3) **Kamenev** and **Zinoviev lost** their **positions** as the **heads** of the **Moscow** and **Leningrad Soviets** respectively.

Stage Three — The **Duumvirate** against the **United Opposition**

Zinoviev and **Kamenev** joined forces with **Trotsky** to form the **United Opposition**. Their **aims** were the **same** as before — a policy of **Permanent Revolution** and an **end** to the **NEP**. But **Stalin** and **Bukharin** were ready for them.

1) The **Duumvirate accused** the **United Opposition** of **factionalism** and **used Lenin's ban** on **factions** against them.

2) The **United Opposition** were **prevented** from speaking at the **1927 Party Congress** which **Stalin** had once again **filled** with his own **supporters**.

3) **Kamenev** and **Zinoviev** were forced to make **humiliating apologies** to **remain** in the **party**.

4) **Trotsky refused** to **apologise**. He was **expelled** from the **party** and **sent** into **exile** in **Central Asia**.

Stalin's Victory (1924-1928)

Stalin was so good at manipulating his opponents that his rivals never really stood a chance against him. Make sure you learn the four stages of Stalin's rise to power so that you can refer to it in the exam without getting muddled up.

Stage Four — Stalin against the Right Opposition

Bukharin **did well** out of his **partnership** with **Stalin**. He **replaced Zinoviev** as **Chairman of Comintern** (an organisation which promoted the global spread of communism) and **Kamenev** as head of the **Moscow Soviet**. But, **Stalin turned** on his last remaining rival.

The crisis was also partly caused by rumours of a foreign invasion which led peasants to hoard their grain.

1) In **1927-28** there was a **grain procurement crisis** due to a **shortage** of **grain**. The **NEP** allowed peasants to sell their **grain** to the **government**, through grain procurement organisations, or to **private traders** (**Nepmen**). The **government** set **low grain prices** — so the peasants **hoarded** their **grain** in the hope of **forcing prices** to **rise**.

2) The **NEP** was **blamed** for the shortage of grain because it didn't allow for state control of the peasants. **Despite** the **unpopularity** of the **NEP** within the party, **Bukharin remained** a **strong supporter** of it.

3) But in **1928**, **Stalin** stunned Bukharin by proposing to **end the NEP immediately** and **implement** a policy of **collectivisation** of **agriculture** and **rapid industrialisation** through a **Five-Year Plan** (see page 15).

4) Stalin's economic policies were **almost identical** to **Trotsky's**, so the **leaderless Left Communists** supported Stalin. Furthermore, Stalin **appealed** to the **majority** of **communists** who **hated** the **NEP**.

5) **Bukharin** was **popular**, but he **wasn't** as **shrewd** as **Stalin** and he was **outmanoeuvred**. **Bukharin** was **removed** from the **party leadership** and **Stalin** was left to **become** the new **vozhd** (boss) of the **USSR**.

Stalin Won because he was the Best Politician

There are **many reasons** why Stalin became the **new leader** of the USSR, but these are the **most important**:

- Stalin's enemies **seriously underestimated** him — they called him 'Comrade Card Index' because they thought he was **just** an **administrator**. However, **Stalin** used his **administrative role** to gain a **huge amount** of **power**.
- **Trotsky** became **isolated** after Lenin's death and he had **many enemies**. The **Triumvirate** formed to **defeat** Trotsky, and when he tried to **fight back** they used their combined **power** and **influence** to undermine him.
- Trotsky took decisions that made it seem he was **strangely reluctant** to **become** the **next leader**. In **1922**, **Lenin** offered him the role of **Deputy Chairman of Sovnarkom** (a body like a cabinet of ministers) — a position that would have strengthened his chance of becoming Lenin's **successor**. But he **refused**.
- **Stalin** had a very **strong base** in the **party**. **Trotsky** had the **support** of the **Red Army**, but this was **taken away** from him when he **lost** his position as **Commissar for War**. **Kamenev** and **Zinoviev** were **only** strong in **Moscow** and **Leningrad** respectively and **Bukharin** had **no major support** in the **party**.
- Stalin **outmanoeuvred** his **opponents** with his **making** and **breaking** of **alliances**. He **teamed up** with a **rival** for as long as he needed them to **attack someone else**, and he **dropped** them when their **opponent** was **defeated**.
- Stalin was also **flexible** with his **policies**, and he **appealed** to **both** the **Right** and **Left** wings of the party.

Practice Questions

Q1 Pick the reason you think is the most important in explaining why Trotsky failed to become the new leader of the Communist Party. Explain your choice.

Exam Question

Q1 Why was Stalin able to defeat his main opponents to become the new leader of the Communist Party? [30 Marks]

Stalin blew his opposition away...

Stalin's rise to power is pretty impressive and quite complicated. If you can nail down the events covered in these two pages then it'll really help you in the exam. The most tricky thing to remember is how Stalin used alliances to pick off his different rivals.

Introduction to Section 2

Some more dates, important people and historical terms for you to learn. Come on, you know you love it really...

This section deals with **Stalin's economic** and **social policies** in the **years 1928-1941**. Here's what you should know:

- The **collectivisation** of **agriculture** was **introduced** from **1928**. It gave the Communist Party **greater control** over the **countryside**. However, **collectivisation** caused the **deaths** of **millions** of **people** through **famine**.

- Between **1928** and **1941** three **Five-Year Plans** were **introduced** which **transformed** the **USSR's industry** and **strengthened** its **economy**. **Heavy industry** made **rapid advances**, but **consumer goods** were **always scarce**.

- **Stalin's social policies ended** the **experimentation** of the **1920s**. The party stressed the **importance** of the **family** within society and **strict discipline** was **imposed** in **schools**. There were **vigorous campaigns** mounted **against religious groups** in the USSR.

Learn the **Key Dates** of **Stalin's Revolution**

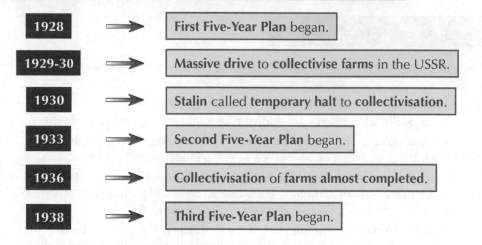

1928 ➡	**First Five-Year Plan** began.
1929-30 ➡	**Massive drive** to **collectivise farms** in the USSR.
1930 ➡	**Stalin** called **temporary halt** to **collectivisation**.
1933 ➡	**Second Five-Year Plan** began.
1936 ➡	**Collectivisation** of **farms almost completed**.
1938 ➡	**Third Five-Year Plan** began.

© Mary Evans Picture Library

Joseph Stalin

Important People in this Period:

- **Alexei Stakhanov** — a miner in the Donbass region, made famous by Soviet propaganda.
- **Alexandra Kollontai** — an influential feminist in the Communist Party.

Make sure you know what these **Historical Terms** mean

- **Gosplan** — The State Planning Committee. It set targets for the Five-Year Plans.
- **Stakhanovite movement** — Created in honour of Alexei Stakhanov to reward hard-working workers.
- **The 'Great Retreat'** — The name given by some historians to Stalin's policy of promoting the family and ending the party's liberal policies for women.

- **Zhenotdel** — The women's department of the party. It was set up in 1919 by Alexandra Kollontai.
- **Komsomol** — The Young Communist League set up for men and women aged 15-25.

Transforming the USSR

Now that Stalin was the new leader of the Communist Party he was able to bring in the policies that he believed would create 'Socialism in One Country'. This section will look at Stalin's successes and failures in achieving his aims.

Stalin wanted the USSR to *Industrialise Very Quickly*

The period **1928-1941** has been called the **second communist revolution** because it saw **major changes**. In **1931** Stalin gave a **speech** in which he stated that the **USSR** was "**fifty** to a **hundred years behind** the **advanced** [western] **countries**". He warned that they needed to "**close** the **gap within ten years**" or the USSR would be "**crushed**".

Stalin believed that the **best way** to make this **massive jump** in **development** was to **introduce** new policies for **both agriculture** and **industry** which would **work together**.

Plans for Agriculture

- **Collectivisation** would **increase** the **output** of **foodstuffs**, especially **grain**.
- This would provide **stable food supplies** for the **towns**.
- **Surplus** grain would then be **exported** so that the USSR could afford to buy the **essential machinery** needed for Stalin's ambitious **industrial plans**.
- Collectivisation would give the **party greater control** over the **countryside** and **eliminate** the **kulaks**.

Plans for Industry

- **Five-Year Plans** would be introduced to **industrialise** the country at **great speed**.
- These would **increase** the numbers of the **proletariat**, the **traditional supporters** of the **Communist Party**.
- The USSR's **industry** would provide **improved technology** that would make **farming** more **efficient**.

Farming in the USSR was *Inefficient*

As Stalin wanted to **rapidly** increase **development** in the USSR, he **needed** to **address** the **long-standing problems** with **agriculture** in the country:

1) **Farming techniques** in the USSR **hadn't** changed much for **hundreds** of **years**.
2) Most farmers tended **small plots** of land, and grew little more than enough to **feed** their **families**, with only a small **surplus** being **sold** on to **feed** the **towns** and **cities**.
3) Many farmers **couldn't** afford **machines** such as **tractors** or **combine harvesters**. They used **old-fashioned** farming implements such as **wooden ploughs**.
4) The **large** and **efficient estates** owned by the **nobles**, the **church** and the **monarchy** were **divided up** after the **October Revolution**. This created **millions** of **smaller, inefficient** farms.
5) The government found it **hard** to **collect food taxes** from the **huge number** of **farms** in the country.
6) Peasants were growing **less surplus** food for the **people** in the **towns**. This created **food shortages**, and **rationing** had to be introduced.

Stalin believed the **Five-Year Plans** would **only work** if the **farms** produced **enough food** to **feed** the **proletariat**. **Collectivisation** gave him greater **control** of **agricultural production**. It also gave him **control** over the **peasants**.

Practice Questions

Q1 Write a paragraph to explain why Stalin believed that reforming agriculture would speed up industrialisation of the country.

Q2 In no more than 50 words explain why farming in the USSR was inefficient before Stalin's reforms.

Stalin's plans — they turned out to be a peasant surprise...

The USSR was lagging behind the major powers and Stalin wanted to reverse this as quickly as possible. Make sure you know how Stalin planned to improve agriculture and industry before you plunge into learning about collectivisation and the Five-Year Plans.

The Collectivisation of Agriculture

Collectivisation gave Stalin control of agricultural production which meant he didn't have to use the hated method of grain requisitioning to feed the workers. Having said that, collectivisation wasn't exactly very popular either.

The **Grain Procurement Crisis** led to **Collectivisation**

The **grain procurement crisis** of **1927-28** gave Stalin the opportunity to **introduce collectivisation**.

1) In **1927** there was a **significant shortage** of food available for the towns. The **government** was paying **very low** prices for **grain**, so the **peasants** started to **hoard** their **harvests** in hope that **prices** would **rise**. Grain hoarding was also caused by **rumours** of a **foreign invasion** — peasants **stockpiled** their **grain** in case of **war**.

2) **Stalin** decided to solve the problem by introducing **grain requisitioning**. **Soldiers** and the **secret police** visited villages and **confiscated grain** wherever they could.

3) This policy **improved supplies**, but in **1928** there was **widespread resistance** to the confiscations.

4) The government realised it **couldn't** continue **grain requisitioning** indefinitely. **Stalin** put forward his plan for **collectivisation**.

Collectivisation meant **Big Changes** to farming in the USSR

1) **Collectivisation** meant that **peasants** had to **give up** their **land**, **home**, **animals** and **farming equipment** to the **state**. **Small farms** were **grouped together** into a larger **collective farm** called a **kolkhoz**.

2) Each year the **government** would take a **quota** of **food** — usually **40%** of the farm's **total output**. The **rest** was **shared** out **among** the **peasants** and their **families**.

3) In some cases a **sovkhoz** (state farm) was set up. Sovkhoz farmers were **paid** a **wage** to work on the farm.

4) **Private ownership** in the **countryside** and **private trading** of **food** were **abolished**.

Collectivisation had **Disastrous Consequences**

Stalin **rapidly increased** the number of **collective farms** between the **summer** of **1929** and the **spring** of **1930**. However, **speedy collectivisation** caused **many problems**:

1) The peasants **didn't** want to **hand over** everything to the **state**, so they **killed** and **ate** their **animals**, **burned down** their own **homes** and **destroyed** their **farming equipment**.

2) The **drastic actions** of the **peasants** made the **food shortages** even **worse**.

3) At the **end of 1929**, **25 000 workers** were sent from the towns to **force the peasants** to **join collective farms**. Those peasants who **refused** were **thrown off** their **land**.

4) By **March 1930**, Stalin realised that **rapid collectivisation threatened** the country's **economy**. He wrote an **article** in **Pravda**, called '**Dizzy with Success**', which **blamed local officials** for the **chaos** in the **countryside**.

5) **Collectivisation ceased** and **many** peasants **left** the **collective farms**.

The **Pause** in **Collectivisation** Didn't Last Long

Stalin was **determined** to **collectivise** the **farms** in the **USSR** — so he **restarted** the **process** in **1931**.

By **1934, 70%** of **all farms** had become **collective farms** and the process was **virtually complete** by **1936**.

The Collectivisation of Agriculture

The policy of collectivisation had a devastating effect on the countryside. Food production fell sharply and millions of people died of starvation. Collectivisation also increased Stalin and the Communist Party's grip over the countryside.

Agricultural output *Dropped Massively*, which caused *Terrible Famine*

1) **Grain production fell** from **73.3** million tonnes in **1928** to **67.6** million tonnes in **1934**.
2) **Livestock** supplies **collapsed** — the number of **cattle** nearly **halved** between **1928** and **1932**. Peasants **slaughtered** their **animals** rather than hand them over to the state. **Many animals** that were handed over **died** through **neglect**.
3) The **kulaks suffered** the **most** under collectivisation. In **1929**, **Stalin** announced his intention to "liquidate the kulaks as a class". **Thousands** were **executed**, sent to **labour camps** or **exiled** to **Siberia**. However, **eliminating** the **kulaks removed** some of the USSR's **best farmers** and made it **harder** for the **collectivised farms** to be **successful**.
4) **Collectivisation** led to a **major famine** in the USSR. The farmers in **Ukraine** had been **resistant** to **collectivisation**, so Stalin **cut off** food supplies to the region and **confiscated** all the **grain**. It's **estimated** that the famine **killed 10 million** people across the USSR.

The famine in Ukraine is known as the Holodomor (murder by starvation).

Collectivisation Helped the Five-Year Plans

1) The **collective farms** provided a **steady supply** of **food** for the **towns** without the use of **grain requisitioning**. This meant the **proletariat** could be **fed**.
2) Food **exports increased**, **despite** the **fall** in **agricultural output**. This meant the **USSR** could afford to **import** more **machinery** to **help** the **Five-Year Plans** (see pages 18-21).
3) The collective farms required **fewer peasants** to farm them, so **millions** of **peasants moved** to the **towns** and **worked** in the **factories**. This increase in labour **boosted industrial output**.

Collectivisation Increased the Party's Control Over the Countryside

1) Collectivisation saw **churches converted** into **barns** or **clubs** for the **peasants**, and priests weren't welcome on collective farms. This **helped** the **Communist Party** because the **Orthodox Church** was **opposed** to the **communists**.
2) Collectivisation **enabled** the **government** to have **direct control** over the **countryside**. This **advanced** the policy of **Socialism in One Country**, which called for the **Communist Party** to tighten its grip **over** the **USSR** so that **reforms** could be made.
3) During collectivisation, **Stalin's hold** on the **party** was **strengthened**. Those who **opposed Stalin**, like **Bukharin**, **lost** their **positions** in the **party** and were **replaced** by men who were **totally loyal** to **Stalin**.

There were **some improvements** in the **countryside**, including the building of new hospitals and schools. **Machine and Tractor Stations** (MTS) were **established** which gave farmers access to **mechanical equipment** in **exchange** for a **share** of their **produce**. However, the **cost** of **renting** the **tractors** was **very high** and there was an **agent** of the **secret police** posted at every MTS to keep an eye on the farmers.

Practice Questions

Q1 Make a list of the problems that collectivisation caused.

Q2 In what ways did collectivisation help Stalin's ambitious plans for rapid industrialisation?

Collectivisation was pretty awful for peasants...

Killing your animals, burning down your own home and destroying all your equipment — Soviet peasants weren't very happy, and with good reason. Stalin's collectivisation of farms made life for peasants very unpleasant and caused a catastrophic famine.

Stalin's Five-Year Plans (1928-1941)

Stalin's Five-Year Plans were hugely ambitious, but then you don't become the leader of a massive country without a little bit of ambition. The Five-Year Plans were the centrepiece of Stalin's domestic policy — you need to know them well.

The **Five-Year Plans** were **Crucial** to the **Success** of the **USSR**

1) The **Communist Party** was traditionally the **party** of the **proletariat**. Stalin hoped that the **expansion** of **industry** would **increase** the **size** of the **proletariat** and therefore create **more** loyal party members.

2) The USSR was the **only** communist state in the world. Stalin was **convinced** that its enemies would try to destroy it. He felt that only an **economically** and **militarily strong USSR** could defend itself.

3) The **NEP** was **becoming** increasingly **unpopular**. Many **new** party members, who were recruited during the **Lenin Enrolment** (see page 9), believed that it **wasn't** helping to **create** an **equal society** because it had **encouraged** the **growth** of the **Nepmen** (urban traders who benefited from the NEP) in the **towns** and the **kulaks** in the **countryside**.

4) The **NEP** had been **successful** in helping the **economy** to **recover after** the **Civil War**, but by **1928** **economic progress** was **slowing** and the NEP **wasn't delivering** the industrialisation the USSR **needed**.

When **Stalin demanded** the **rapid industrialisation** of the USSR, he received **widespread** and **enthusiastic support**. **Many** party members felt that an **advanced** and **equal society** could be **achieved** with the **Five-Year Plans**.

The **Five-Year Plans** called for a **Command Economy**

Stalin had to **introduce** a **command economy** (which is where production levels and prices are set by the government) to make the Five-Year Plans work. To do this he turned to **Gosplan** — the State Planning Committee.

- **Gosplan set targets** for **each industry**.
- These **targets** were **sent** to **each region** of the **country**.
- The **targets** were then **sent** to **each factory**, **mine**, etc.
- Factory managers **set targets** for **every worker**.
- But Gosplan **didn't** say **how** the **targets** should be **achieved**. This was **left** to **individual managers** to decide.

"Now to execute my cunning Gooseplan."

During the **first** Five-Year Plan **various targets** were **suddenly increased** to often **unrealistic levels**. **Managers** had to try to **adapt** to the new production targets **very quickly**.

The First Five-Year Plan — October 1928 to December 1932

1) The **first plan** was aimed at developing **heavy industries**, such as **coal**, **iron**, **steel**, **oil** and **heavy machinery**. Stalin believed these were the **building blocks** of an **advanced industrial economy**.

2) **New industrial plants** were built to the **east** of the **Ural Mountains** where they would be **safe** if the USSR was **invaded** from the **west**. **Uzbekistan** and **Kazakhstan** were **developed economically** for the **first time**.

3) **New cities** were built from **scratch**. The **most** important was **Magnitogorsk**, which went from being a **small village** in **1928** to a **town** of **250 000** people in **1932**. However, the people **lived** and **worked** in **terrible conditions**.

4) **Electricity** was **vital** to the **first plan** — the **massive hydroelectric Dnieprostroi Dam** was built on the **River Dnieper**.

5) **Tractor factories** were built in **Stalingrad** and **car factories** in **Moscow**. **Canals**, built by prisoners, **connected** **Moscow** with the **River Volga**, and **Leningrad** with the **White Sea**.

During the Second World War Magnitogorsk produced half of all the steel needed to build the USSR's tanks.

In **1929**, Stalin **announced** that the **first plan** would be **completed** in **four years**. **Posters** were put up with the **slogan** '2 + 2 + the enthusiasm of the workers = 5'.

Stalin's Five-Year Plans (1928-1941)

The first Five-Year Plan was a great success, despite not reaching its unrealistic targets. The second plan continued the first plan's development of heavy industry — with an extra emphasis on improving the USSR's agricultural output.

The **First** Five-Year Plan **Didn't** meet its **Targets** — but it was **Impressive**

The table below shows you the level of **output** of **five major industries** in **1928** and the level they rose to in **1932** after the **first plan**. It also gives the **targets** that **Stalin set** for this period.

	1928 Output	1932 Output	1932 Target Output
Electricity (billion kWh)	5.05	13.4	17.0
Coal (million tonnes)	35.4	64.3	68.0
Oil (million tonnes)	11.7	21.4	19.0
Pig-iron (million tonnes)	3.3	6.2	8.0
Steel (million tonnes)	4.0	5.9	8.3

Although **oil** was the **only** industry to **exceed** its **target**, the general **increase** in **output** during the **first** Five-Year Plan was very **impressive**. However, the **unrealistic targets** that were set meant that **managers** were more **concerned** about the **quantity** of what they produced, rather than the **quality**.

It's hard to find accurate figures for the first plan because many records were falsified.

The **Second** Five-Year Plan — January 1933 to December 1937

The second Five-Year Plan **maintained** a **focus** on **heavy industry**, but also **strengthened other areas** of the economy.

1) To **improve** the **agricultural output** from **collectivisation**, more **mechanical agricultural equipment**, such as **tractors** and **combine harvesters**, were built.

2) **Railways** and **canals** were built **between** the **new centres** of **industry** to ease the transport of goods and raw materials.

3) There were **some attempts** to **increase** the **supply** of **consumer goods**, but they **remained** a **low priority** for Stalin. New **boots** and **shoes** became **nearly impossible** to obtain.

4) **Stalin** was interested in building '**showpiece**' developments for **propaganda purposes**. The **Moscow Metro**, with its **chandeliers** and **marble statues** of **heroic workers**, was built during the second plan.

5) The **new factories** built during the **first plan** became **fully functioning** during the **second plan**. These **contributed** to the **second plan's success** as they greatly **increased** output in these years.

6) A **system** of **wages** was **introduced** which **rewarded** those who made **greater efforts** than others.

Practice Questions

Q1 Make a list of reasons why Stalin introduced the Five-Year Plans.

Q2 In no more than 50 words, explain how the USSR tried to increase industrial output in the period 1928-1932.

Q3 What were the priorities of the second Five-Year Plan?

The party was right behind the Five-Year Plans...

Tractor factories, massive hydroelectric dams and canals built by prisoners — Stalin really got Soviet industry growing. It certainly made the Communist Party happy — they thought the plans would spell the beginning of a new era.

Stalin's Five-Year Plans (1928-1941)

Stalin learnt some lessons from the first Five-Year Plan — he set more realistic targets for the second. The third Five-Year Plan, like the second, aimed at increasing production of consumer goods, but it was rudely interrupted by an invasion.

A **Propaganda Campaign** was used to try to **Increase Output**

The **party used propaganda** to **encourage workers** to **work harder**.

The Stakhanovite Movement

- In **1935**, it was reported that a **miner** from the **Donbass region**, **Alexei Stakhanov**, had mined **102 tonnes** of **coal** in a **six-hour shift**. This was **fourteen times** his **allotted quota**.
- Soon after, it was reported he'd **broken** his record — mining **227 tonnes**.
- He received many awards, and the **Stakhanovite movement** was **created** to **reward workers** who **exceeded** their **quotas**.
- In **1988**, a Soviet newspaper **revealed** his **achievements** were **exaggerated**.

An intensive period of working was known as 'storming'. It was a very inefficient way of improving output.

The **Second** Five-Year Plan had **Good Results**

The table below shows you the level of **output** of **five major industries** in **1932** and the level they rose to in **1937** after the **second plan**. It also gives the **targets** that **Stalin set** for this period.

	1932 Output	1937 Output	1937 Target Output
Electricity (billion kWh)	13.4	36.7	38.0
Coal (million tonnes)	64.3	128.0	152.0
Oil (million tonnes)	21.4	28.5	46.8
Pig-iron (million tonnes)	6.2	14.5	16.0
Steel (million tonnes)	5.9	17.7	17.0

Some industries fell **well short** of their **target output level**. But despite this, the **figures** still **show** that in the major industries output **significantly increased** in this period.

The Third Five-Year Plan — January 1938 to June 1941

Priorities changed during the course of the **third plan**, as **war** with Nazi Germany **seemed increasingly likely**.

1) The third plan began with a **focus** on producing **consumer goods**, such as **radios** and **cars**.
2) However, Stalin feared that **war** would **break out** between the **USSR** and **Nazi Germany**. Consequently, the third plan became **increasingly** devoted to the **production** of **aircraft**, **tanks** and **weapons**. By **1940**, a **third of the government's budget** was **spent** on the **USSR's military**.
3) The Nazi **invasion** in **June 1941** meant that the **third plan** only lasted **three** and a **half years**.
4) During the third plan, **output** grew **very little** in many industries. This was partly due to Stalin's **purges** (see pages 27-29), which led to the **imprisonment** or **execution** of many **skilled workers**.
5) **Internal passports** were created to **control** the **movement** of **people** in the USSR. This **stopped** workers from **regularly changing** their **jobs** and **ensured** that **factories** had a **stable workforce**.

Stalin's Five-Year Plans (1928-1941)

The Five-Year Plans helped the USSR to become a major industrial power. This meant that although the USSR hadn't closed the gap between itself and the advanced western nations entirely, it could now fight a big war. Which was handy.

The **Five-Year Plans** were a **Great Success** for **Stalin**

The Five-Year Plans had a **major impact** on the USSR **economically**, **socially** and **politically**.

Economy and Industry

1) Between **1928** and **1940**, the **USSR** was **transformed** from a largely **agricultural country** into one of the **leading industrial powers** in Europe. However, **production** was still very **inefficient**.

2) The **1930s** was the **decade** of the **Great Depression**, and most countries suffered **falling production** and **high unemployment**. The **USSR experienced** the **opposite** of this. The **success** of the Five-Year Plans was a great **propaganda triumph** for the Communist Party.

3) **Major projects** such as **Magnitogorsk** and the **Moscow Metro** impressed **Soviets** and **foreigners** alike.

4) Stalin worried that without **rapid** industrialisation the **USSR** would be "**crushed**". However, in the **Second World War** the USSR had the **industrial power** to **defeat** the Nazis. This seemed to **prove** Stalin was **right**.

USSR's Society

1) In the period **1928-1941** life was still **tough** for **most people** in the **USSR**. **Wages weren't high** and there were **few consumer goods** available in the shops.

2) The **population** of **towns** and **cities** more than **doubled** between **1928** and **1941** as peasants flocked to **towns** to find **work** in **industry**. Furthermore, by **1940 women** accounted for **40%** of the **labour force**.

3) Many Soviets, especially **young people**, were prepared to **work very hard** to make the **plans succeed**. They were **convinced** by Stalin's **propaganda** that they could **achieve** the **seemingly impossible**.

4) This period saw **more investment** in **health care** and **education**. The number of **doctors** in the USSR **nearly trebled** and **everyone** was **entitled** to **free medical assistance**. **Illiteracy** was **greatly reduced** and **more people** went to **university**. **Paid holidays** were also introduced.

Communist Party's Control

1) In **1928** the **Communist Party** was **well established** in the **cities**, but had **little power** in the **countryside**.

2) By **1940** the combined effect of **collectivisation** and the **Five-Year Plans** had **destroyed** the old way of life in the **towns** and **countryside**. The USSR was **transformed** into an **industrialised** nation and the **party** had **dramatically increased** its **control** over the **entire country**.

Practice Questions

Q1 Why did the Communist Party exaggerate the achievements of Alexei Stakhanov?

Q2 Why did Stalin's priorities change during the third Five-Year Plan?

Q3 Give some examples of why the Five-Year Plans might have been considered a success for Stalin.

Exam Question

Q1 How successful were the first three Five-Year Plans in achieving their aims in the years 1928-1941? [30 Marks]

Glossary

Great Depression — a period of serious economic hardship that affected most countries in the world

The Five-Year Plans brought the USSR forward...

For the exam you need to be aware of the successes and failures of the Five-Year Plans, so make sure you know what they are. You could test your knowledge of the plans by writing a mini-essay on the aims and results of each of the Five-Year Plans.

Stalin's Social Policies

The Communist Party's policies towards women changed dramatically between 1917 and 1936. The party went from being laid-back about women's role in society to being really controlling. Shockingly, Stalin had a hand in that.

At first the party had **Radical Policies** for **Women**

1) The Communist Party's **official policy** was that **men** and **women** were **equal**.
2) In **1919** a **women's department** of the party, called the **Zhenotdel**, was created under the **leadership** of **Alexandra Kollontai**. The Zhenotdel proposed **very liberal policies** towards women, such as:
   - Simple methods of **divorce**
   - The spread of **female literacy**
   - Allowing **abortion** on demand
3) The Zhenotdel did its utmost to **undermine** the **institution** of the **family** because it saw it as a **symbol** of **prerevolutionary oppression**.

The **Radical Policies** for **Women** had **Mixed Results**

Pros
1) More women **entered** the **workforce**. In **1928** women accounted for **less than 20%** of the **industrial workforce**, but this figure had **risen to 40%** by **1940**.
2) **Educational opportunities** for **women** were **improved** so that by **1940 over half** of all **university students** were **women**. This created **new career opportunities** for women in fields such as **medicine** and **engineering**.

Cons
1) By the **late 1920s more** than **half** of **marriages** were **ending** in **divorce**. Instead of liberating them, the liberal policies on the family left many women **impoverished** and **unable** to **raise** their **children**.
2) The **break-up** of so many **marriages** led to the **growth** of **gangs** of **orphans** and **unwanted children** in **large cities**. These gangs **contributed** to a **rise** in **crime rates**.
3) Women made little progress within the Communist Party itself. Women formed only a **small proportion** of the **party membership** and, with the exception of **Alexandra Kollontai**, they **failed** to **reach** the **highest positions** within the party.

Stalin's own **industrial** and **agricultural policies** had also **weakened** family ties.
Many **families** were **uprooted** and **forced** to move **hundreds** of **miles** to **find work**.

Stalin began to promote **Traditional Values**

1) The growing **breakdown** of **society** in the USSR led Stalin to introduce changes which have become known as the **'great retreat'** in family policy.
2) The **Zhenotdel** had already been **closed** in **1930**, but **Stalin** wanted to **go further** and **promote** the **family** as the **foundation** of a **socialist society**.
3) He issued **laws** in **June 1936** which were designed to **strengthen** the **family**:

1) **Child support payments** were **increased** substantially, and there were strong **financial incentives** introduced for **families** to **grow larger** and **stay together**.
2) **Most abortions** were **outlawed** and **divorces** were made **hard** to get and **very expensive**.

In this period, women were given **new opportunities** to **find work** and have **careers**. However, Stalin's **promotion** of the **family** and **social stability** meant that **women** were **expected** to **balance** their **traditional roles** as **wives** and **mothers** with having a **job**.

Stalin's Social Policies

Stalin's reforms were aimed at creating a strong socialist state in which the people were taught to be loyal citizens. Not content with ruling the country with an iron fist, Stalin wanted the people to love him as well. He was that insecure...

Stalin needed to **Reform** the USSR's **Failing Education System**

1) The party **experimented** with the **education system** in the **1920s** — with a focus on **vocational learning** and **political indoctrination** and away from **formal education** and **examinations**. This caused a **fall** in **standards**.

2) As part of the so-called **'great retreat'**, **Stalin** put a strong **emphasis** on **examinations** and **strict discipline**. The school curriculum focused on **literacy** and **numeracy**, which were necessary to create **skilled workers**, and on **history**, which would help create **loyal citizens**.

3) **Rule 1** of the **20 Rules of Student Behaviour** stated, "It is the **duty** of each child to **acquire knowledge** persistently so as to become an **educated** and **cultured** citizen, and to be of the **greatest possible service** to his **country**."

Children and young people were indoctrinated in youth organisations

- The **Young Pioneers** was established for **children under** the age of **fifteen**.
- The **Young Communist League** (Komsomol) was for **young men** and **women** aged **15-25**.
- These institutions were **used** by the **party** to **spread propaganda**, especially **against** the **kulaks** and in **favour** of **collectivisation**. Members **pledged** their **loyalty** to **Stalin**.

Religion was **Attacked** by Stalin

The **destruction** of **religious organisations** and **religious beliefs** was a **long-term aim** of the **party**. **Lenin** believed that **atheism** and **communism** were "inseparable". Under **Stalin religious believers** suffered **frequent persecution**.

1) In **1929** a **law** was passed that made it **illegal** to carry out any **religious activities** apart from in **places** of **worship**, such as **churches**, **synagogues** or **mosques**.

2) During the **1930s** there were many **violent attacks** on **Orthodox churches** and their **priests**. Out of **over 150 bishops** active in **1930**, only **12 hadn't** been **imprisoned** by **1939**.

3) **Muslims**, especially in **Central Asia**, were **vigorously persecuted**. Communities were **banned** from practising **Islamic religious law** and **women** were **encouraged** to **not** wear the traditional Muslim **veil**. **Fasting** in the month of **Ramadan** was **condemned** and **Muslims** were **forbidden** from making the **pilgrimage** to **Mecca**.

4) **Jews** continued to suffer from **anti-Semitism**, just as they had done under the Tsars.

5) Despite the persecution, religious belief **didn't disappear**. Many **congregations** met in **secret**. In **Central Asia** there were **frequent outbreaks** of **violent resistance** in the **Islamic communities**.

6) In **1941 persecution** of the **Russian Orthodox Church** was **eased** following the **Nazi invasion** — Stalin tried to **unite society** in the USSR around **traditional Russian values**.

Practice Questions

Q1 Why did Stalin change the USSR's policies towards women and education?

Q2 Give some examples of how religion was suppressed between 1928 and 1941.

Exam Question

Q1 To what extent did the position of women in Russia improve in the years 1928 to 1941?   [30 Marks]

Control — you must learn control...

When you're revising Stalin's social policies, keep in mind the ways in which they benefited him or his party. Stalin's policies were focused on keeping and maintaining control over the country, and if anything threatened that then it would be suppressed.

Introduction to Section 3

Here it is — it's my friend and yours... the 'Summary of a Section' page. You know the drill — key dates, important people and historical terms. Learn them and love them.

Here's a **Quick Summary** of **Section Three**

This section deals with **Stalin's purges** of the **1930s** and the **use** of **culture** and the **arts** in the **service** of the **state**. Here's some useful information:

- **Repression** of the **Soviet people** had been a **feature** of life ever **since** the **October Revolution** of **1917**.
- In the years **1934-1938 repression** became **more intense** with the **purges** and the **Great Terror**. Stalin used the **purges** firstly to **rid himself** of **enemies within** the **party**, before **targeting ordinary people** and the **army**.
- The **purges** saw the **further development** of the **system** of **labour camps** which **imprisoned millions** of **people**.
- **All aspects** of **artistic** and **cultural life** had to **follow guidelines laid down** by the **government**.
- Stalin used a **personality cult** to **promote himself** as the **wise** and **heroic leader** of the **people**.

Learn the **Key Dates** of the **USSR** as a **Totalitarian State**

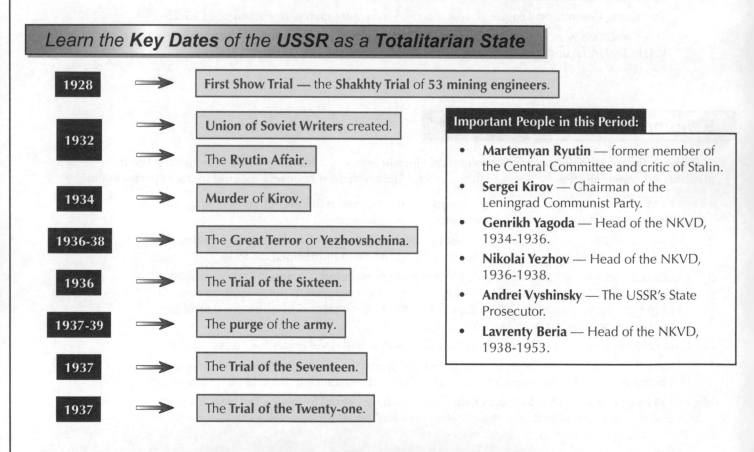

| 1928 | → | First Show Trial — the Shakhty Trial of 53 mining engineers. |

| 1932 | → | Union of Soviet Writers created. |
| | → | The Ryutin Affair. |

| 1934 | → | Murder of Kirov. |

| 1936-38 | → | The Great Terror or Yezhovshchina. |

| 1936 | → | The Trial of the Sixteen. |

| 1937-39 | → | The purge of the army. |

| 1937 | → | The Trial of the Seventeen. |

| 1937 | → | The Trial of the Twenty-one. |

Important People in this Period:

- **Martemyan Ryutin** — former member of the Central Committee and critic of Stalin.
- **Sergei Kirov** — Chairman of the Leningrad Communist Party.
- **Genrikh Yagoda** — Head of the NKVD, 1934-1936.
- **Nikolai Yezhov** — Head of the NKVD, 1936-1938.
- **Andrei Vyshinsky** — The USSR's State Prosecutor.
- **Lavrenty Beria** — Head of the NKVD, 1938-1953.

Make sure you know what these **Historical Terms** mean

- **Yezhovshchina** (the Great Terror) — A period of widespread purges that targeted anyone who was seen as a threat to Stalin. It was directed by Yezhov.
- **NKVD** — USSR's secret police. It replaced the Cheka.
- **Show Trials** — Scripted public trials used for propaganda. The defendants were forced to make confessions and the outcome of the trials was pre-decided.

- **Socialist Realism** — A realistic and optimistic style of art and literature promoted by Stalin and the party.
- **Personality Cult** — Where someone uses propaganda to create an idealised image of themselves. It's often used to create loyalty.
- **Gulag** — The name given to the forced labour camps across the USSR.

Totalitarianism in the USSR

The USSR in the 1930s has been described as a totalitarian state. A totalitarian state is one where the government aims for total control of the society, politics and culture in a country.

The USSR had many **Characteristics** of a **Totalitarian State**

The **previous section** described how Stalin imposed **state control** over:

- economic life in the cities and the countryside
- education
- family life

However, to **increase** his **control** over the USSR, Stalin wanted to **remove opposition** to his **rule**. He **achieved this** through **severe repression** (see pages 27-29), by **creating** a **personality cult** (see page 31) and by **strict control** of **artistic** and **cultural life** (see pages 30-33).

Lenin had used **Repression** to keep **Control**

Stalin **wasn't** the first leader to use **repression** to **maintain** a **firm grip** on the **USSR**. **Lenin** used repression **successfully** to **crush opposition**.

1) In **1917** Lenin set up the **Cheka**, a **secret police** force. Their task was to **maintain communist rule** by **any means necessary**.

2) The Cheka unleashed the **Red Terror**. **Aristocrats**, members of the **middle class** and **priests** were rounded up and **killed**.

3) During the **Civil War**, the **Cheka** went into **villages** to **confiscate grain** from the **peasants**. The **grain** was used to **feed** the **Red Army**.

4) By the **early 1920s, labour camps** were being set up to house people accused of **anti-communist activities**.

Stalin used **Show Trials** to create **Fear**

From **1928** Stalin decided to hold a number of **show trials** to assert his authority. Show trials were **carefully scripted** public trials where the **defendants** were **forced** to **make confessions**, and the **outcome** of the **trial** was **already decided**. The trials were **broadcast** on the **radio** and **reported** in the **newspapers** to **strike fear** into the **people**.

There were **three** important show trials between **1928** and **1933** that you should know about:

Shakhty Trial 1928	**Menshevik Trial 1931**	**Metropolitan-Vickers Trial 1933**
Fifty-three engineers from the **Donbass region** were accused of **industrial sabotage** and **conspiring** with **Germany**. **Forty-nine** were **convicted** and **five** were **executed**.	Former members of the **Mensheviks**, who were working as **economists** for the government, were **accused** of **undermining** the **first Five-Year Plan**.	**Six British engineers** working in Russia for **Metropolitan-Vickers** were arrested and charged with **spying** and **sabotage**.

Practice Questions

Q1 In what ways did Lenin use repression to keep control?

Q2 What were show trials?

Lots of trials and tribulations — just Cheka you know the facts...

You won't be tested on Lenin's methods of repression, but you should know that repression was used before Stalin took power. You will need to know about Stalin's show trials, so make sure you learn these three, and there will be more to come later.

The Purges

Stalin's popularity in the Communist Party seemed to be in decline and his policies were increasingly unpopular. It appeared that his position as supreme leader of the party was under threat. Unsurprisingly, Stalin wasn't having that...

Opposition to Stalin was Growing

1) In the **early 1930s** there were **growing concerns** about the **effect** of Stalin's **economic policies**. Many believed that **collectivisation** had been introduced **too quickly** and **too brutally**, and that the **industrialisation** of the USSR had been done **without** enough **concern** for its **effects** on the **lives** of the **people**.

2) **Several** members of the Communist Party were beginning to **question Stalin's leadership**. Some members were **considering** the possibility of **replacing Stalin** as **General Secretary**.

3) Stalin also faced a major **external threat** after **1933** — Nazi Germany. **Hitler** detested communism and he often spoke of the **inevitability** of a **war** between Germany and the USSR.

Ryutin Challenged Stalin's Authority

Stalin's **authority** was **undermined** by the **Ryutin Affair**.

The Ryutin Affair — 1932

1) In **1932, Martemyan Ryutin**, a **former member** of the party's **Central Committee**, called for a "**fresh start**" in **economic policies**, and wrote that **Stalin** was the "**gravedigger** of the **revolution**".

2) Stalin demanded his **immediate arrest** and **execution**, but his party colleagues **successfully** argued **against** Ryutin's **execution**.

3) **Ryutin** was sentenced to **ten years** in **prison**, but he was **eventually executed** in **1937**.

4) The **Ryutin Affair** showed that Stalin still **didn't** have **full control** of the **party** or the **government**. This might explain why Stalin's **earlier purges** struck the **Communist Party** itself, especially those that Stalin **believed** were his **enemies**.

Kirov seemed to be a Likely Alternative to Stalin

Sergei Kirov was the **Chairman of the Leningrad Soviet** and a **leading figure** in the Communist Party. In **1934**, he appeared to be a **threat** to Stalin's dominance.

1) **Kirov** was **handsome, charismatic** and **popular** with party members. He was **Russian, unlike Stalin**, which further **increased** his **appeal** to party members.

2) Kirov was a **hard-line** communist, but he'd been **linked** to **moderates** in the party who were **unhappy** with some **shortcomings** of the **first Five-Year Plan** and had **argued** for a **better standard of living** for **industrial workers**. He'd also **argued against** the **execution** of **Ryutin** in **1932**.

3) After Stalin's death, reports began to emerge that at the **1934 Party Congress**, the '**Congress of Victors**', **Stalin** had received **over** one hundred **votes against** his **re-election** to the party's **Central Committee**, whereas only a **handful** had **voted against Kirov**. These stories suggest that there was **some resistance** to **Stalin's rule**, and that **Kirov** was **popular enough** to have been a **possible challenger**.

The exact voting figures for the Congress of Victors were suppressed.

4) On **1st December 1934, Kirov** was **murdered** in his office in Leningrad by **Leonid Nikolayev**. It's **unclear** whether **Stalin ordered** Kirov's **murder**, but he used the incident to **unleash** a **purge** against his **opposition**.

The Purges

Stalin unleashed a brutal campaign of purges against the Communist Party in an attempt to purify it of any opposition to his control. However, the purges soon meant targeting anyone who was regarded as a threat to Stalin's authority.

Kirov's Assassination allowed Stalin to Purge his Enemies

1) **Stalin** claimed that the **assassination** of **Kirov wasn't** the work of a **lone gunman**, but was part of a **widespread conspiracy** against the government. Stalin used this as an **excuse** to **arrest** and **execute** his **enemies** in the party.

2) The **Leningrad Party** was among the **first targets** of Stalin's purge against the party. A **purge** of the **party's leadership** was undertaken by **Genrikh Yagoda**, the **head** of the **new secret police** (the **NKVD**) — **40 000** people in **Leningrad** were **arrested** and **removed** from the city.

3) Stalin also **purged** the **delegates** of the **Congress of Victors**, many of whom **hadn't voted** for his **re-election**. During the next **three years**, **over half** of the **delegates** were **arrested** and many of these were **executed**.

4) Yagoda was **replaced** in **1936** by **Nikolai Yezhov**, who was very **loyal** to Stalin. Yezhov's purges **didn't** just target enemies in the party, but **targeted anyone** who Stalin believed was a **threat**. The period during which **Yezhov** was **head** of the **NKVD** (1936-1938) is known as the **Great Terror** or **Yezhovshchina** (which means Yezhov's rule).

Stalin's Purge eliminated High-profile Communist Party members

There were **three** major **show trials** between **1936** and **1938**:

The Trial of the Sixteen — 1936

1) Among the sixteen who were charged were **Kamenev** and **Zinoviev**.
2) The defendants were **accused** of:
   - being **members** of the **Trotskyite-Zinovievite Counter-Revolutionary Bloc**
   - **conspiring** to **murder Kirov**
   - **undermining** the **Five-Year Plans**
3) **All** of the accused were **forced** to **confess** their 'crimes' and they were **all shot**.

The Trial of the Seventeen — 1937

1) The accused included **Karl Radek** and **Georgy Pyatakov**, who had been **close allies** of **Lenin**.
2) Among other things, they were **charged** with **spying** for **Nazi Germany**.
3) **Radek** made a **confession** which **saved** his **life**, but he **incriminated** his friend, **Bukharin**.
4) **Thirteen** of the defendants, including **Pyatakov**, were **executed**.

The Trial of the Twenty-one — 1938

1) **Bukharin, Alexander Rykov**, who'd been a **member** of the **Right Opposition**, and **Yagoda** were put on trial.
2) The defendants were **accused** of **treason** and **sabotage**. **Bukharin** was also **accused** of **plotting** to **kill Lenin**.
3) They were **all executed**.

Practice Questions

Q1 In no more than 50 words, summarise why Stalin might have feared that he would be forced out of power in 1934.

Q2 Why did Stalin purge the Communist Party?

Stalin wasn't going anywhere — he knew how to take Kirov the opposition...

Stalin used the purges to wipe out his old rivals who had struggled against him to succeed Lenin. They were all executed on fabricated charges. Revise the three trials carefully so that you know who was involved, the charges and the results.

The Purges

I'm really sorry, but it doesn't get any cheerier. After rooting out his enemies in the party, Stalin's purges spread to the army and to ordinary Russians. The purges stopped during the Second World War, but they were continued afterwards.

Stalin **Purged** the **Red Army**

1) Stalin **didn't trust** the **Red Army** — he feared that they would launch a **military coup** against him.
2) **Most** members of the **armed forces** came from **peasant families**, which had been **badly affected** by **collectivisation**.
3) In **1937 Andrei Vyshinsky**, the **State Prosecutor**, announced that a **"military-Trotskyist conspiracy"** against Stalin had been **uncovered**. He claimed it was **led** by **Marshal Tukhachevsky**, a **hero** of the **Civil War**. Tukhachevsky was **charged** and **shot** with **seven** other **alleged conspirators**. His arrest and trial were kept **secret** until after his death to **avoid** causing **unrest among** the **soldiers**.
4) Between **1937** and **1939**, **half** of the **officers** (approximately **35 000** men) were **imprisoned** or **shot**, and **replaced** with **inexperienced officers**. This **seriously weakened** the **Red Army**.
5) In the **air force**, only **one** senior commander **survived** the **purges**.

The **Great Terror** tore society apart

1) Between **1936** and **1938** the Russian people lived in a **permanent state** of **fear** under the **Yezhovshchina**.
2) There was **chaos** in **factories**, **mines** and **collective farms** as **workers** and **peasants** rushed to **denounce one another**. In some cases, **members** of the same **family denounced each other** to the **authorities**.
3) The **Great Terror** coincided with the **third Five-Year Plan**, but so many members of **Gosplan** had been **purged** that the **plan** was **issued** in **draft form only**. During this period, the **purging** of so many workers **slowed industrial growth**.

Pavlik Morozov

- It was **reported** that a **13-year-old** peasant boy, **Pavlik Morozov**, **denounced** his **father** for **corrupt dealings** in running a **collective farm**.
- His **father** was **imprisoned** but Pavlik was **murdered** soon afterwards. It was **claimed** that he was **killed** by **members** of his **own family**.
- The party used Pavlik as a **propaganda figure**, portraying him as an example of a **good young communist** who **put** the **party before** his **own family**.

Purges **Continued** after the **Second World War**

The worst of the purges were **over** by **1938**. **Yezhov** was **arrested** in **1939** and **executed** the following year. His replacement as **head** of the **NKVD** was **Lavrenty Beria**. Beria was **responsible** for **two** more **significant purges**:

1) In **1945 Russian prisoners** of **war** began to be **repatriated** (sent back to Russia). **Stalin** and **Beria** believed that they were **potential traitors** and sent them to **labour camps** where they worked as **slave labour**.
2) In **1949** there was a new **Leningrad purge**. It was **limited** to **party members**, and there were **several hundred arrests**.

Beria had an early success as head of the NKVD when an agent managed to assassinate Trotsky in August 1940.

In **1953 Stalin** became **convinced** that a **'Doctors' Plot'** had been hatched against him by **Jewish doctors**. He was preparing to unleash a **massive purge** against Russia's **Jewish population**, but he **died** in **March** of that year.

The Purges

As terrible as the purges were, some people actually thought that they were a good thing. Stalin was only one man, and it was impossible for him to kill so many Soviets unless enough people believed that it was the right thing to do.

The Purges were a Success for Stalin

By **1938** the **purges** had **achieved** their **main objectives**:

1) **All** of Stalin's potential **political** and **military opponents** had been **destroyed**.
2) He had **total control** over the **party**.
3) He had **succeeded** in **creating** an **atmosphere** of **fear** in the country. Between **1938** and **1953** no **individual** or **group** dared to **challenge Stalin's leadership** of the USSR.

Stalin's Success came at a Great Price

The **human** and **economic cost** of the **purges** was **massive**.

1) The **exact figures** of those who were **imprisoned** in **labour camps** or **died during** the **Great Terror** are **unknown**. However, it's **estimated** that between **7** and **8 million** people were **arrested** in this period, of which **1 million** were **executed** and **most** of the rest were sent to **labour camps**, **usually** in **Siberia**. Approximately **2 million died** in the **labour camps**, where the prisoners worked as **slave labour**.

The labour camps are often called 'Gulags', which comes from the Russian acronym for the agency in charge of them.

2) The **USSR's industry** was **badly affected** by the **purges** — it **lost** many of its **best specialists** and **managers**. Factories **lost** a **large proportion** of their **workforce**. The **purges** made it **impossible** to **achieve** the **targets** of the **third Five-Year Plan**.
3) The **education system** was severely **undermined** as **universities** and **schools** lost **thousands** of **professors** and **teachers**.
4) The **army** had been so **weakened** by the **purge** of its **officers** that it **struggled** to **defeat Finland's small** but **well-trained army** in the **Winter War** of **1939-40**.

Some people believed that the Purges were Necessary

Despite all of the **suffering** that the **purges caused**, there were **some** who **welcomed** them.

- Many **communists** wanted Stalin to **eliminate** the last of the country's **class enemies**, such as the **Nepmen** and the **kulaks**. They believed that the **enemies** of **progress** had to be **removed** to **create** an **advanced** and **equal society**.
- Communist Party **propaganda convinced** many **Soviets** that there were **traitors** within Soviet society who were **determined** to **undermine** the **country** or **sell it out** to **foreign powers**.
- Others simply **used** the **purges** as an **opportunity** to **settle grudges** or to **improve** their **own position** in **society**.

Practice Questions

Q1 Why did the Communist Party promote the story of Pavlik Morozov?

Q2 What effects did the purges have on society in the USSR?

Exam Question

Q1 To what extent did the purges strengthen Stalin's control over the USSR? [30 Marks]

Glossary

coup — a sudden seizure of power.

Stalin's purges make most other murderous dictators look like amateurs...

Finally, we've come to the end of the miserable purges. For the exam, you need to know the reasons why Stalin decided to carry out the purges and what effect they had on politics and society in the USSR. So unfortunately you've got to you learn this stuff.

A Totalitarian Culture

Stalin's control over the USSR was not achieved through fear alone, but also through the manipulation of culture. He made sure that all aspects of culture followed very strict guidelines and conformed to Socialist Realism.

Soviet Art was Revolutionary in the 1920s

The **1920s** was an **era** of **experimentation** in **Russian culture**.

- In the **1920s**, **artists**, **musicians** and **architects** had some **freedom** to **experiment** with their work. The **culture** of this period was a **reaction against** the **elites** in **society** who had **dominated** culture under the **Tsars**.
- Russia's **literature** was **dominated** by the **Russian Association of Proletarian Writers** (RAPP) which was created in **1925**. The organisation **promoted realism** in **literature** and wanted writers to concentrate on the **everyday activities** of **ordinary people**.
- The **realism** that **RAPP** called for was **influenced** by the novel *Cement* (1924), written by **Fyodor Gladkov**. The story focuses on an **ex-Red Army soldier**, **Gleb Chumalov**, who **works** in a **cement factory**. **Gleb** leads a crusade **against corruption** and **incompetence** in the factory and **brings** it up into **full production**.
- During the **first Five-Year Plan**, many **novels** were written with **similar themes**, where one individual **triumphed** against **overwhelming odds** to **fulfil** the **targets set** by the **plan**.
- There was also **experimentation** in **architecture**. **Vladimir Tatlin's** plan for a **Monument to the Third International** was a very ambitious project. He designed a **400m** high **tower** made of **iron**, **glass** and **steel**, which would become a **symbol** of a **new age**. It proved to be too **impractical** and was **never built**.

Stalin Ended the Experimentation in Culture

In the **1930s** Stalin **decided** to **end** the **experimental period** in **culture** and the **arts**.

1) Stalin wanted **culture** to **serve** a **political purpose**. He intended to use **culture** to **promote socialism** and the **achievements** of the **Five-Year Plans**. This led to the introduction of **Socialist Realism**.
2) During the **19th century**, **much** of **Russian culture** was **realist** in form, which means that the **writers** and **painters** of the period produced works that **showed society** as it **really was**, both **good** and **bad**.
3) **Socialist Realism** was **different** because the government wanted **all artists** and **writers** to **produce** works which **glorified** the **struggle** of the Soviet people through **revolutions**, **civil war**, **industrial development** and the **collectivisation** of **agriculture**. **Art, literature** and **music** were meant to **promote socialism** and **party policies**.

Socialist Realism was another Method of Control

Stalin saw artists as "**engineers** of the **human soul**". He used artists to **influence** how the people **thought** and **behaved**.

1) **Socialist Realist** art and writing was made to **make Russians** feel **optimistic**. Its style was **simplified** so that **ordinary people** could **appreciate** it. **Abstract** art **wasn't permitted**.
2) **Paintings**, **sculptures** and **books** focused on the importance of the **hero**, a **role model** for others to **follow** and **imitate**.
3) By **exaggerating** the **positives** of a socialist society and **creating heroes** for the people to **follow**, Stalin was using **art** to make Russians **feel** and **act** in a **certain way**.
4) **Socialist Realist writing** was, to some extent, **similar** to Gladkov's *Cement*, but the **language**, the **characters** and the **plots** were **much simpler** than **Gladkov's**.

A 1935 Painting of Stalin at the hydroelectric complex at Ryon.

A Totalitarian Culture

Stalin's personality cult was similar to the Cult of Lenin, created after Lenin's death. Stalin wanted people to be loyal to him and he set about encouraging this by rewriting history. A tactic you probably don't want to adopt in the exam.

The **Cult** of **Lenin** was **Sidelined** by the **Cult** of **Stalin**

Stalin had **enthusiastically promoted** the **Cult** of **Lenin** (see page 9), but in the **1930s** he began to **develop** his **own personality cult**.

- In **1938** two books were published — the *Short Course of the History of the All-Union Communist Party* and the *Short Biography of Stalin*.
- These books **rewrote** the **history** of the **party** and **emphasised Stalin's contribution** to the **growth** and **success** of the party.
- **Stalin's role** in the **October Revolution** and the **Civil War** was **greatly exaggerated**, but Trotsky's role was **completely ignored**.
- Stalin's **genius** was referred to **daily** in the **press** and on the **radio**.
- **Propaganda posters** appeared which **showed Stalin** as being **god-like**. Many of them also featured **Lenin** to show that **Stalin** was **continuing** his **predecessor's work**.

Stalin's purges led to several party leaders being erased from history. Photographs were altered and paintings were repainted to remove condemned traitors.

The **Cult** of **Stalin** was **Everywhere**

By '**worshipping**' their **leader**, the **Cult of Stalin** gave **ordinary Soviets** a **link** to their **government**.

1) **Towns**, **cities** and even **mountains** were named in **honour** of **Stalin** — the city of **Tsaritsyn** was renamed **Stalingrad**.
2) Many aspects of **popular culture**, including **music** and **film**, were used to **promote** Stalin's cult.
3) **Children** were **taught** from a **young age** to be **loyal** to **Stalin** and to **idolise him** (see page 23).
4) **Stalin's birthday**, **18th December**, was turned into a **national celebration**.

Stalin was **Portrayed** as a **Hero**

1) Stalin **successfully** led the USSR to **victory** over **Nazi Germany** in the **Second World War**.
2) His **success** became the **central feature** of the **propaganda** used to **promote him** after the war.
3) Stalin was also **portrayed** as a **world leader** because he was part of the **important negotiations between** the **allies** during and after the war. His **prestige** as a world leader **increased** when large parts of **Eastern Europe** were added to the **Soviet Union** in the 1940s.

Practice Questions

Q1 Describe the changes in Soviet culture during the 1920s.

Q2 How did Stalin see the role of culture in society?

Q3 What were the main features of Socialist Realism?

Q4 How did Stalin promote his own personality cult?

Exam Question

Q1 How successful was Stalin in establishing a personal dictatorship in the years 1928-1945? [30 Marks]

Stalin always made it personal...
On the 'to do' list of horrible dictators, creating a personality cult is usually pretty high up, and Stalin was no different. He worked hard to put across an idealised image of the country and of his leadership at a time when the USSR was gripped by the Great Terror.

Culture Under Stalin

There were some pretty strict rules and regulations on the work of artists in this period. They had to produce work which was easy to understand for the masses, had clear heroes and villains, and advanced the cause of socialism.

Socialist Realism Influenced the Literature of this period

In **1932** the **Russian Association of Proletarian Writers** was **closed down** and was **replaced** by the **Union of Soviet Writers**. This organisation **followed** the **ideas** of **Socialist Realism** with **great enthusiasm**.

These are **three** famous **Socialist Realist authors** of this **period**:

Mikhail Sholokov

1) **Sholokov** wrote **two** popular **novels** which centred on a **hero** who **struggled against adversity**.
2) *And Quiet Flows the Don* (1934) and *The Don Flows Home to the Sea* (1940) **follow** the **life** of a **Cossack family** who lived by the **River Don**. Sholokov shows the family **involved** in the **great events** in Russia **from before** the **First World War** to the **end** of the **Civil War**.
3) The books were **very popular** both **inside** the **USSR** and in **Europe** and **America**. In **1940**, **Sholokov** was **given** the **Stalin Prize for Literature**.

Nikolai Ostrovsky

1) **Ostrovsky** wrote *How the Steel Was Tempered* (1934), whose hero was **Pavel Korchagin**.
2) The book **depicts** the **First World War**, the **Revolutions** of **1917**, the **Civil War** and the **Five-Year Plans**, and **how** they **affected Pavel's life**. Pavel believes that the **greatest thing** you can do is **dedicate** your **life** to the **liberation** of **humankind** — by helping the **communist revolution**.

Maxim Gorky

1) **Gorky** was a **very influential** writer in this period.
2) He **left Russia** in **1921** after he became **disillusioned** with the **October Revolution** and with **Lenin**, who he felt was **just as bad** as the **Tsars**.
3) **Gorky returned** in **1932** at **Stalin's invitation** and was **given** a **hero's welcome**. He was a **big supporter** of **Socialist Realism**, but he **fell under suspicion** after **Kirov's death** in **1934**
4) He **died unexpectedly** in **1936** — there were rumours he was **murdered** by the **NKVD**.

Music was Strictly Regulated

Socialist Realism extended to the **world** of **music**. **Popular music** of the **1930s** was **constantly optimistic** and **positive** about the **country's achievements since** the **October Revolution**. Some **famous songs** of the **1930s** were —

- 'Song of the Motherland'
- 'We Will Be Like Lenin'
- 'Three Tank Drivers'

Dimitri Shostakovich

1) **Experimentation** in **music** was **suppressed**, a **famous example** being **Dimitri Shostakovich's 1934 opera**, *Lady Macbeth of Mtsensk*, which was **criticised** in **Pravda** for being **too confusing** for **ordinary Soviets**.
2) **Stalin went** to **see** the **opera**, but **left before** the **end**.
3) However, **Shostakovich saved** his **career** with his highly acclaimed 1941 *Leningrad Symphony*. It was composed while the **Germans** were laying **siege** to **Leningrad**, and its **style** has been **compared** to **Socialist Realism** — because the piece is **stirring** and **patriotic**.

Culture Under Stalin

You won't need an in-depth knowledge of what books, songs and films were produced in this period for the exam, but it's important to know some examples to show how Stalin influenced culture.

Paintings and Sculpture emphasised the Realistic

Paintings and **sculpture** were made as **realistic** as possible to **reflect Socialist Realism's insistence** that **all** the **arts** should be **understood** by the **whole population**.

- The **Moscow Metro** was **built** in the **1930s** and many stations **displayed huge frescoes** and **sculptures** of **ordinary** Russian **workers**, **peasants** and **soldiers**.
- **By 1940 enormous statues** of both **Lenin** and **Stalin** were **erected** in virtually every **town** and **city across** the **USSR**.
- Many paintings showed **Stalin** or **Lenin** meeting with **ordinary Soviet people**. The **setting** and the **people** in the paintings were meant to look **realistic** — so that the picture was **almost** like a **photograph** of a **real event**.

Films Glorified Russia, the October Revolution and Stalin

The **most famous** film director of this period was **Sergei Eisenstein** — his **work** was **heavily scrutinised** by **Stalin**.

Sergei Eisenstein

- **Eisenstein's** film, *October*, produced in **1927** to **commemorate** the **tenth anniversary** of the **October Revolution**, was **partially censored** by **Stalin** to **remove Trotsky** from the **film**.
- He also made *Alexander Nevsky*, which was a **film** about an **invasion** of **Russia** by **German Teutonic Knights** in the **13th century**, and their **total defeat** by **Russian** forces **led** by **Alexander Nevsky**.
- The script of *Alexander Nevsky* played on **fears** of a **war** between the **USSR** and **Germany**. **Stalin suppressed** the **film after** he **signed** a **non-aggression pact** with the **Nazis** (see page 35), but it was **restored** to Soviet **cinemas** soon **after** the **German invasion** of the **USSR** in **1941**.

Films were also **used** to **develop** the **personality cult** of **Stalin**.

1) These films **weren't based** on **reality** — they **exaggerated** the **part played** by **Stalin** in **major events** such as the **October Revolution** and the **Civil War**.
2) The **1945** film *The Fall of Berlin* included **one scene** where **Stalin landed** in **Berlin** and **delivered** a **speech** to a **multinational crowd** about the **need** for **peace**. This event **never** took place.

Architecture became Less Radical

1) In the **1930s**, there was a **turn away** from **experimental architecture**. Stalin wanted buildings that looked **less radical**, and were influenced by more **traditional** styles of architecture.
2) A **Stalinist style** developed that's been labelled by some as '**wedding cake architecture**' — where **imposing buildings** rise up in **layers** or tiers, like a wedding cake. Examples include the **Seven Sisters skyscrapers** in Moscow, which were built in the 1940s and early 1950s.

Practice Questions

Q1 Give an example of a Russian writer in this period and describe how Socialist Realism influenced their work.

Q2 Why did Stalin control art in the USSR so tightly?

Exam Question

Q1 To what extent did Stalin use art as a form of social control in the years 1928 to 1945? [30 Marks]

The Song of Stalin...

As a special treat, here's the popular hit from 1937, the 'Song of Stalin' — 'We carry this name with us everywhere / It opens all horizons and distances / We will go into any battle behind you / Our banner, our victory, our Stalin!' And repeat. Forever...

Introduction to Section 4

It's quick, it's smart, it gets you loads of marks — it's the Summary Page. Learn these key dates, important people and historical terms and you've got a one-way ticket to Successville. It's just lovely in the autumn — you've got to see it.

Here's a **Quick Summary** of **Section Four**

This section deals with the **invasion** of the **USSR** in **1941**, the **USSR's eventual victory** and the **emergence** of the **USSR** as a **superpower**. Here's some information to get you started:

- **1941** was a **disastrous year** for Stalin. On **22nd June 1941**, German forces **invaded** the **USSR**. The **German invasion** led to the **loss** of **much** of **western Russia** and **Ukraine**, and by the end of the year **Moscow** and **Leningrad** were both **threatened** by **German forces**.
- **Soviet resistance grew** from **1942** and the **Red Army** won **important victories** at **Stalingrad** and **Kursk**. In **1945** Soviet troops entered Germany and **captured Berlin**.
- The **wartime economy** was **controlled** by **Stavka** and **Gosplan**. **Lend-Lease** made an **important contribution** to the **USSR's victory, especially** in **improving** the **Red Army's transport** and **communications**.
- After **1945** the **USSR controlled most** of **Eastern Europe** and was **actively involved** in **promoting** its **aims** and **beliefs** in **many parts** of the **world**.

Learn the **Key Dates** of the **USSR** in the **Second World War**

Aug 1939 ⟹	**Molotov-Ribbentrop Pact signed.**
1941 ⟹	**Operation Barbarossa launched.**
1941-45 ⟹	Period of **Lend-Lease**.
1942-43 ⟹	**Battle** of **Stalingrad**.
1943 ⟹	**Battle** of **Kursk**.
May 1945 ⟹	The **capture** of **Berlin**.
1946 ⟹	**Fourth Five-Year Plan** began.
1949 ⟹	The **USSR tests** an **atomic bomb**.
1953 ⟹	The **death** of **Stalin**.

Important People in this Period:

- **Vyacheslav Molotov** — Soviet Foreign Minister, 1939-1949 and 1953-1956.
- **Joachim von Ribbentrop** — Germany's Foreign Minister, 1938-1945
- **Marshal Zhukov** — Head of the Soviet forces during the Second World War.
- **Nikita Khrushchev** — Stalin's successor as leader of the USSR.

Make sure you know what these **Historical Terms** mean

- **Operation Barbarossa** — The code-name for Nazi Germany's invasion of the USSR.
- **Stavka** — Committee made up of the high command of the Red Army. Had the power to dictate economic policy for the benefit of the war effort.
- **Lend-Lease** — Policy where the USA supplied goods to the USSR free of charge until the end of the war.

- **Molotov-Ribbentrop Pact** — A non-aggression treaty signed by the Nazis and the USSR. It also included a secret deal to split Eastern Europe.
- **De-Stalinisation** — A policy, implemented by Khrushchev, which denounced Stalin's personality cult and his use of purges.
- **Superpower** — A country with massive economic and military strength, with the ability to influence countries around the world.

The USSR in the Second World War

The Second World War proved to be the making of the USSR — the country survived a devastating war and emerged as a victorious superpower. The USSR wasn't going to get pushed around by the playground bully any more.

The **USSR Signed** a **Non-Aggression Pact** with the **Nazis**...

1) Stalin was worried about the **Anti-Comintern Pact** of **1936** whose main signatories were **Germany** and **Japan** (**Italy** signed in **1937**). The **Comintern** was an organisation controlled by Moscow which aimed at **spreading communism globally**. The pact showed a developing **alliance** against **communism** and the **USSR**.

2) Stalin **tried** to make an **alliance** with **Britain** and **France** to **protect** the USSR, but they refused. After this **setback** Stalin ordered his foreign office officials to try to **make** a **deal** with the **Nazis**.

3) In **August 1939** German **Foreign Minster Ribbentrop** and his **counterpart Molotov** negotiated the **Molotov-Ribbentrop Pact**. The pact **agreed** that **neither country** would **invade** the **other** and it **secretly** carved up **Eastern Europe** between the **two** powers.

... but **Hitler** still wanted to **Invade** the **USSR**

1) Hitler viewed the **Slav peoples** of the USSR as 'Untermenschen' — **subhuman**. His **racist** beliefs gave his troops a **free hand** to **kill** Soviets **indiscriminately** or to **enslave** them to **work** for the **German war effort**.

2) Hitler wanted '**Lebensraum**', or '**living space**', to Germany's **east**. He wanted to **clear Ukraine** and **White Russia** (now Belarus) of its **inhabitants** so that **German families** could be **settled** there.

3) The **USSR** had **vast amounts** of **raw materials** and **natural resources** that Hitler wanted — for example, **Ukraine** produced a **large amount** of **grain** and the **Caucasus region** was **rich** in **oil**.

Hitler used '**Blitzkrieg**' against the **USSR**

On **22nd June 1941** the Germans began **Operation Barbarossa** — the **invasion** of the **USSR**. The **German army** was **divided** into **three groups** whose **objectives** were — to **attack Leningrad** in the **north**, **Kiev** and **Moscow** to the **centre**, and the **Black Sea area** and **Stalingrad** to the **south**.

1) The German army used their '**Blitzkrieg**' tactic. '**Blitzkrieg**' means '**lightning war**', and it involved **large numbers** of **infantry** and **tanks**, **supported** by **enormous air power**, moving in a **fast** and **coordinated assault** on the enemy.

2) The German attack in the **north** reached **Leningrad** by the **end** of **September** but was **unable** to make any further **progress**. **Hitler** ordered his troops to **lay siege** to the city. The **siege lasted** for **nearly three years**.

3) The German army reached **Moscow** by **December 1941**, but when the **winter** set in, the **German advance stalled**. The **German soldiers** had **little winter clothing** and it was **so cold** their **weapons** became **useless** and the **diesel** in their **tanks** and **trucks froze**. **Fierce Soviet resistance** and **inadequate supplies** forced the **Germans** to **retreat**.

4) The assault **towards** the **south almost reached** the **Black Sea**, but was **halted** by a **strong division** of the **Red Army**.

- By the **end** of **1941** Germany **controlled** a **huge area** of the **USSR** and about **45%** of the **country's population**.
- The **USSR lost access** to its **large grain supplies** from **Ukraine**, along with **areas** it **depended on** for much of its **coal** and **steel production**.
- **Hundreds** of **thousands** of **Soviet soldiers** had been **killed**, **wounded** or **taken prisoner**. The USSR also **suffered substantial losses** of **tanks**, **aircraft** and **heavy artillery**.

Practice Questions

Q1 Why did Stalin want to sign a non-aggression pact with Nazi Germany?

Q2 Give some reasons why Hitler wanted to invade the USSR.

Stalin and Hitler — Best Friends Forev... er... for two years...

Stalin ignored intelligence reports that showed the Germans were about to attack. He didn't believe that Hitler would invade before Britain was defeated and so he made little preparation to stop an invasion. The Red Army wasn't ready for the German attack.

The USSR in the Second World War

Operation Barbarossa — named after the cursed captain of the 'Black Pearl' (not really...) — was devastating, but the USSR survived and from 1942 they were able to fight back and slowly drive the Germans out of the Soviet Union.

The USSR began to gain the Upper Hand

Despite the **German successes**, the **USSR** had managed to **avoid defeat** and it **slowly** turned the tide of the war.

1) After **disappearing** from public view in the early days of the war, **Stalin returned** to provide **effective leadership**. Stalin **stayed** in **Moscow**, even though it seemed the city would **fall** to the **Germans**, and his presence **boosted** the **morale** of the **Soviet soldiers**.

2) The Soviets used a **'scorched earth'** policy as they **retreated** — **sabotaging roads** and **bridges**, **destroying food supplies** and **damaging communication lines** — making it **harder** for the **German army** to get **supplies** as it **advanced**.

3) The **Nazis' racism** hurt Germany's war effort. Many Soviets **didn't** like Stalin and were willing to **support** the **Germans**, but they **changed their minds** when the **Germans treated** the **people** under their control **brutally**.

4) **Rumours** of atrocities **spread** to the rest of the **USSR**, and most **Soviets** realised that they had to be prepared to **fight to the death** in what Stalin called the **'Great Patriotic War'**.

The Battle of Stalingrad was the Beginning of the End for the Nazis

1) In **1942 Hitler** ordered an **attack** on **Stalingrad**. His aim was to seize the city to allow the **German army** to push **south** and **capture** the **oil fields** of the **Caucasus region**.

2) Within a **few months** the **fighting** had reached the **city's suburbs**. Stalin ordered **every able-bodied citizen** to be supplied with a **rifle** so that they could **defend** the **city**.

3) By **November**, German troops had **entered** the **city** and **weeks** of **fierce house-to-house fighting** followed. The Germans **almost captured** the **whole city** before the tide turned.

4) **Soviet forces** under **Marshal Zhukov** began a **counter-attack** outside of the city, **cutting off** the **German supply lines**. They **trapped** most of the German army **inside** the **city**.

5) **Surrounded** and **starving**, the German soldiers eventually **surrendered** on **2nd February 1943**. 90 000 German soldiers were **taken prisoner**.

6) The **victory** at **Stalingrad raised** the **morale** of the **Red Army** and **humiliated** the **Germans**.

Kursk was a Decisive Victory for the Red Army

1) In **1943**, the **Germans** deployed around **700 000 men** at **Kursk**, **supported** by roughly **2700 tanks**. The **Red Army** had **approximately 1.3 million men** at the battle, with up to **3300 tanks**.

2) After the initial German attack, the **Soviets** mounted a powerful **counter-attack** which **smashed** the **German line**. The **Germans** were **forced** to **retreat**.

3) Kursk was the **largest tank battle** of the war and it was a more **decisive victory** than Stalingrad. There were **massive losses** on **both sides**, but the **German army** in the **east** had been **broken**.

The Fall of Berlin Concluded the War in Europe

1) By **1945** the Soviets began their **final assault** on **Germany** itself.

2) **Soviet troops entered Berlin** in **April 1945**.

3) On **2nd May 1945, Berlin surrendered** and six days later, **8th May**, the **war** in **Europe** was **over**.

4) It's **estimated** that **between 20 and 30 million Soviets died** during the war, and it **caused massive social upheaval** in the **USSR** (see pages 37-38).

The USSR in the Second World War

Unfortunately for the Soviet civilians, their needs came a distant second to the needs of the Red Army. As a result life was very difficult for most people in the USSR, but Stalin tried to cheer everyone up by not persecuting religion for a bit.

Life in the Countryside was Hard

1) The **biggest change** in the **countryside** was that **millions** of **farmers** were **taken from** the **land** to **fight**.
2) The task of **producing most** of the **country's food** was left in the hands of **women**, **children** and those who were **too old** to **fight**.
3) **Conditions** on the **farms** were **grim**. Horses and **tractors** were in **very short supply**, so **teams of women** were often reduced to **pulling** the **ploughs themselves**.

Life in the Towns was also Tough

1) **Despite** the **best efforts** of the **farmers**, **food** was in **desperately short supply** in the **towns**.
2) **Food** was **rationed according** to the amount of **work** that was **done**. **Only** those who **worked** were **given a ration card** — those who **couldn't work** were **left** to **fend** for **themselves**.
3) **Many people** had to **survive** on **less** than the **official daily ration** and **millions starved** to **death**.
4) **Workers** were **expected** to **work seven days** a **week** without **holidays**.
5) **Most homes** were **without electricity** for most of the war.

Stalin Stopped the Persecution of Religion

The **communists** had **attacked religion** throughout their time in power, but Stalin **changed** this **policy** in **1943**.

1) In **1943** Stalin **reopened** many **churches** and **religious schools**.
2) He also **allowed** the **Russian Orthodox Church** to **elect** a **leader**, or **Patriarch**, for the **first time since** the **1917 October** Revolution.
3) In return the **Church agreed** to **support Stalin** and the **government**. It also **preached** in **favour** of the 'holy war' **against** the invading **Germans**.
4) **Religion wasn't** truly **free** — it was **controlled** by **Stalin** and the **party** — but the **reopening** of **churches** gave the intended boost to Soviet **morale**.

Stalin used Propaganda to Strengthen Morale

1) **Stalin's propaganda emphasised** the **defence** of the "**Motherland**" by the USSR's "**brothers** and **sisters**".
2) **Stalin** was shown as a **wise leader** and **military strategist**, **working constantly** for the **defence** of the **Motherland**.
3) A **new national anthem** was **introduced** in **1944**, which **glorified** the **USSR**.
4) **Shostakovich's** *Leningrad Symphony* (see page 32), which was **composed** in the **besieged city**, was **broadcast across** the **USSR**.

Practice Questions

Q1 Why were the battles of Stalingrad and Kursk so important?

Q2 Give three reasons why the USSR was able to defeat Germany in the Second World War.

Have a proper gander at the facts — then learn them...

The fall and rise of the USSR during the Second World War was quite spectacular. The USSR came from the brink of defeat to relentlessly grind down the German army and claim victory. The USSR won at a great cost, but they won, and that's what counts.

The USSR's War Economy

One of the main reasons why the USSR was able to defeat Germany was because they out-produced them.
A command economy and mass production were nothing new to the USSR — thanks to the Five-Year Plans.

The **Germans Captured** a **Large Chunk** of the **USSR's Industry**

By the **end** of **1941** German forces had **overrun** and **occupied** much of **western Russia** and **Ukraine**.

1) **Millions** of **people**, including **specialists** and **technicians**, fell under **Nazi control**.
2) **Huge amounts** of **vital raw materials**, such as the **coal supplies** in the **Donbass region**, were **captured**.
3) The **loss** of **Ukraine** cost the **USSR** its **main grain producing lands**.

Stalin created **Stavka** to **Coordinate** all **Military** and **Civilian Activities**

Stavka was a body made up of the **high command** of the **Red Army**. It was given the **power** to take **any measures necessary** for the **benefit** of the **war effort**. Stavka demanded that the **whole economy** should be **used** for the **war effort**, and it **acted quickly** to **limit** the **invasion's effects** on the **economy**.

1) Between **two** and **three thousand factories** located in the **western** part of the **Soviet Union**, which were **vital** for the **war effort**, were **dismantled** and **moved** by rail **towards** the **east** of the **country**. They were moved **beyond** the **Ural Mountains** where they were **safe** from **German attacks**.
2) **Approximately 25 million** people, **factory workers** and their **families**, were also **moved** to the **east**. They **rebuilt** the **factories** and **restarted production**.
3) The **managers** of **factories** were given far **more freedom** to run their plants than they were during the Five-Year Plans. **Targets weren't set** for **output** — instead **factories** were **urged** to produce as much equipment for the war as they could.
4) Production of **consumer goods slumped** dramatically. The economy **prioritised** the **war**, which meant that **consumer goods** were regarded as an **unnecessary luxury**. It soon became **virtually impossible** to buy **everyday goods**, such as **shoes** and **clothing**.

Central Control of the **Economy** was **Very Successful**

1) By **1942** over half of the USSR's **national income** was spent on the **war**, which was **proportionally** more than **any other** country.
2) The **USSR** was able to produce **arms** and **ammunition** more **efficiently** than the **Germans**. Although the USSR's economy **suffered greatly** from the invasion, the USSR **out-produced** Germany in **weapons**, **tanks** and **planes** by **1943**.
3) Before the war the **majority** of **factory workers** were **men**. However, as millions of workers were **drafted** into the **armed forces**, their places in the workplace were taken by **women** and, as the war progressed, by **young boys**.
4) Even **labour camps** made a **significant contribution** to the **war effort**, producing **millions** of **rounds** of **ammunition** and other supplies for the army, including **rifles**, **uniforms** and **boots**.

Soviet workers assembling a T-34 tank, 1943.

The **USSR's ability** to **out-produce Germany** was a **very important factor** in its **eventual triumph**. It meant that the **Red Army outnumbered** the **Germans** in terms of **tanks** and **aircraft** in **most battles**.

The USSR's War Economy

While the USSR produced most of its own weapons, tanks and aircraft during the war, Lend-Lease helped the Soviets get certain things they couldn't make themselves. It played an important role in the Soviet defeat of the Nazis.

Lend-Lease *Strengthened the* USSR's War Effort

In **March 1941 President Roosevelt** encouraged the **US Congress** to **pass** the **Lend-Lease Act**. This allowed the **US** to **supply goods**, including **military equipment**, to countries who **needed help** with their **war effort**. **Lend-Lease** was, at first, mainly **aimed** at **supplying Britain**, but it was **extended** to help the **USSR after** the **German invasion**.

1) **Very little** reached the **USSR** from the West **until 1943**. Compared to what the USSR produced, **Western support** was **relatively small**, but it was **vital** in **certain areas**.

2) **Radio equipment** sent to the USSR improved the Red Army's battlefield communications. It meant that **troops** could be **directed rapidly** and **efficiently**.

3) **Lend-Lease** provided some of the **vital** raw materials that were in **short supply** (e.g. **aluminium**, **copper** and **coal**) after the USSR's loss of the **Donbass region**.

4) **Specialists** were sent to the **USSR**, and **Soviet technicians visited** the **West** to **study** **techniques** to **improve** the **quality** of **armaments** and **increase production**.

5) **Food production** in the **USSR** had **slumped** since **Germany seized** the **grain fields** of **Ukraine**. **Lend-Lease supplied millions** of **tons** of **food**, including **vast quantities** of Spam. **Khrushchev**, the leader who **succeeded Stalin**, claimed **Spam** was **essential** to the **Red Army's victory**.

The USSR Relied *on* Lend-Lease *for Transport*

1) The **USSR's rail network** was in a **poor condition** in **1942**. **Lend-Lease helped** to **ease** this **problem** with **large shipments** of **track**, **engines** and **wagons** to **transport** both **men** and **supplies**. As a result, **millions** of **troops** could be **moved quickly** to **different parts** of the **Eastern Front**.

2) The **USA** supplied the **USSR** with **approximately 375 000 trucks** and **50 000 jeeps**. These were **very important** in **supplying frontline troops** — they **allowed** the **Red Army** to **move quickly** against the Germans **without losing touch** with their **supply lines**.

3) The **USSR produced most** of its **own tanks** and **aircraft** — it didn't need much of these from the **West**. For example, when it was first introduced, the **Soviet T-34** tank was **more effective** than **most tanks built** in the **West**.

1) Some historians have argued that **Lend-Lease wasn't** crucial to the USSR's **war effort**. But the USSR did **benefit greatly** from the **support** that **Lend-Lease** provided in **feeding** its **troops** and **improving transport** and **communications** across the country.

2) However, after the war, when relations between the USSR and the US had soured, **Stalin** made a point of **playing down** the role of Lend-Lease in the **USSR's victory**.

This book has benefitted from the Lend-Geese scheme.

Practice Questions

Q1 Why did the USSR relocate much of its industry during the war?

Q2 Give some examples of how Lend-Lease helped the USSR's war effort.

Exam Question

Q1 How far was the USSR's economy responsible for the Soviet victory in the Second World War? [30 Marks]

The USSR was flooded with Spam...

But this spam was useful because it didn't inform Stalin that a distant relative had left him 3 squillion roubles for him to collect — once he'd handed over all his bank details. Stalin didn't want to give any credit to foreigners, so his propaganda ignored Lend-Lease.

A New Superpower

For the USSR to be considered a 'superpower' it would have to have a stable domestic society, a strong economy and substantial military power. It also needed to be able to defend its interests and use its influence on a global scale.

The **USSR Emerged** from the **Second World War** as a **Superpower**

1) In **1939** there were **seven countries** which were recognised as **Great Powers** — Britain, **France**, **Germany**, **Italy**, **Japan**, the **USSR** and the **US**.
2) By **1945** Germany, **Italy** and **Japan** had been **defeated** in **war**.
3) **France** and **Britain** were **victorious**, but their **economies** were **badly weakened** and they had **little prospect** of a **quick recovery**.
4) Only the **US** and the **USSR** were **left** as **great** powers with **global importance**.

Soviet Society was Stable

1) In **1945** the USSR was a **one-party state** with **very little freedom** of **speech** or **expression**.
2) The **purges** of the **1930s** had **eliminated** any **threat** to the **rule** of the **Communist Party**, and there was **no one** to **challenge Stalin's position** as **leader**.
3) In **1941** the USSR, and **communism** itself, was in **danger** of being **destroyed** by the **Germans**.
4) **Victory** in **1945 strengthened** both the **USSR** and **communism**. The **USSR** now had **control** over **most** of **Eastern Europe**, which meant that more countries became **communist** (see page 41).

The **USSR's** economy was **Badly Hit** by the war

The **economy** of the **USSR** had **developed rapidly** during the **Five-Year Plans** (**1928-1941**) and was **strong enough** to **out-produce** the Nazis in **military equipment** during the war. But the **war** had caused terrible damage:

1) **Approximately 25 million Soviet citizens** were **killed** during the **war**.
2) **70 000 villages** and **1700 towns** were almost **completely destroyed**.
3) **25 million** people were **left homeless**.
4) **Thousands** of **factories** and **mines** had been **demolished**.
5) The **USSR** had **spent** a **large proportion** of its **wealth** on the **war**.

The **Fourth Five-Year Plan Strengthened** the **Economy**

Despite the **hardships** caused by the war, the **Soviet people** made a **massive effort** after the war to **repair** the **damage**. In **1946** Stalin introduced the **fourth Five-Year Plan** to **restore economic production**.

The Fourth Five-Year Plan 1946-1950

1) The **plan** helped the **USSR's** economy grow **bigger** than it was in **1940**.
2) **Production** in **heavy industry quickly matched** and then **surpassed pre-war levels**.
3) The **amount spent** on the **USSR's** military in **1946** was **greater** than it was in **1940**.
4) **Consumer goods** were **still** in **short supply** and **living standards** remained **low**...
5) ... but the **USSR's economic output** was now **second only** to the **US's**.

A New Superpower

After marching across Eastern Europe and into Germany, the USSR wasn't going to just stop there. The USSR quickly developed a nuclear weapon which meant that it became a truly global power.

The USSR believed in a Strong Military

1) **During** the **war** the **USSR** spent a **larger proportion** of its **national income** on the **military** than **any other country**.
2) **After 1945** the **Red Army** wasn't demobilised. **Millions** of **soldiers** were **stationed across Eastern Europe**.
3) **Military leaders** played an **increasingly important role** in the **government** of the **country**.

In **1945** the **USA** used **two atomic bombs** on **Japan**. Stalin **ordered** Soviet scientists to **develop** a **nuclear weapon**. Thanks to **information** provided by **espionage**, the **USSR** was **able** to **develop** a **nuclear bomb** and **test** it in **1949**.

Eastern Europe fell under Soviet Control

1) In **1945** the **Red Army** marched across **Eastern Europe** on its way to **Berlin**. They claimed that they were **liberating** the **countries** they **passed through** and would **hold free elections**.
2) **Stalin failed** to **keep** his **promises**. By **1948**, **countries** across **Eastern Europe** had Soviet-backed **communist governments**, those most controlled by the **USSR** being **Poland**, **Hungary**, **Romania**, **Bulgaria**, **Czechoslovakia** and **East Germany**.
3) **Soviet influence** in these countries was **strengthened** when they **joined** with the **USSR** and **Albania** to **form** the **military alliance** known as the **Warsaw Pact**.

The USSR Extended its Influence Outside of Europe

1) In **1949 China** became a **communist country** under the **leadership** of **Mao Zedong**.
2) **Stalin** sent **military** and **economic advisers** to **China**. Mao adopted the **Stalinist economic model** of the **Five-Year Plans** and the **collectivisation** of **agriculture**.
3) **Stalin assisted communist North Korea** during the **Korean War** of **1950-53**.
4) Many **colonies** in **Africa** and **Asia developed** strong **liberation groups** which aimed to free them from **colonial rule**. **Communism** was **popular** among these **groups** because it **emphasised equality** and **brotherhood**. **Stalin** sent them **money** and **advisers** to **aid** their **struggle**.

Stalin's Legacy was Attacked by Khrushchev

1) **Stalin** had **widespread popularity** in the **USSR** and **across** the **world** for his part in **defeating** the **Germans**.
2) **Stalin died** in **1953**, and his **body** was placed **alongside Lenin** in the **mausoleum** in **Moscow's Red Square**.
3) **Stalin's successor**, **Nikita Khrushchev**, started a process of **'de-Stalinisation'**. In **1956 Khrushchev denounced** Stalin's oppressive rule, and **revealed** that **Lenin's Testament** had **called** for Stalin's **removal** from power.
4) In **1961 Stalin's body** was **removed** from the **mausoleum** and was **buried** in **Moscow**.

Practice Question

Q1 In what ways did the Second World War affect the USSR's economy?

Exam Question

Q1 How far was the USSR's victory in the Second World War responsible for its emergence as a superpower? [30 Marks]

So that's it — quit Stalin and get revising...

Stalin brutally and ruthlessly turned the USSR into a superpower, but all Khrushchev could do was criticise. There's gratitude for you. Oh well, I suppose you'd better learn how to write some really good essays — head over to Section 5 and 6 and be amazed...

The Exam

Your exam is 'Unit 1 — Historical Themes in Breadth — Option D — A World Divided: Communism and Democracy in the 20th Century'. A bit of a mouthful. Polar bears don't do exams, but if they did, they'd be brrrrilliant...

You have to answer **Two Questions** in **1 Hour 20 Minutes**

1) The exam paper has questions on **seven topics**. You will have **studied two** of them, so you can **ignore** the rest.

2) You need to know the **name** and **number** of the **topics** you have studied, e.g. D4 — Stalin's Russia, 1924-53.

3) **Each** topic has a choice of **two questions** — you only need to answer **one** of them.

4) The exam is **1 hour 20 minutes** — that gives you **40 minutes per question**.

5) **Each question** is worth **30 marks** and so they're both **equally important**.

Great hair gave Tim the confidence to ace his exam.

Don't Rush — **Read** the question and **Plan** your answer

At the start of the Exam

- Look at **both** questions **carefully** and decide which you will find **easier** to answer. Read the **whole question** and not just the key words — the question might be different to what you were expecting.
- Spend about **5 minutes thinking** about what the question is asking you for. Jot down **important points**.

During the Exam

- **Answer the question**. Don't write an answer to a question you've memorised — <u>**answer the question in the exam paper**</u>. If you keep **referring back** to the question in your answer, then you won't get sidetracked.
- Keep an **eye on** the **time**. You'll lose marks if you spend an hour on the first question and only leave yourself 20 minutes for the other one.

At the end of the Exam

- If you have time at the end, **check through** your **answers**. Make any corrections **neat** and **obvious** — it makes it easier for the examiner to see your changes.

The Exam **Also** tests **How** you **Write**

You're writing for **someone else**, so don't make it hard for the examiner to understand what you're saying.

1) Structure your essay in **paragraphs** (see page 45).

2) Write in an **appropriate style**. This is a **formal** exam, so it's **not** a good idea to use slang, chattiness or text speak.

3) The examiner will consider your **spelling** and **grammar** when deciding the mark, so make sure your essay is easy to **read** and **understand**.

4) Use '**history terms**' which link to your module — e.g. **totalitarian**, **Socialist Realism**, **communist**.

5) Write **neatly** — the examiner **can't give** you **marks** if they **can't read** what you've **written**.

You best be usin' proper grammar now — Proper grammar is proper good...

If you didn't already know, the examiner is not your friend — they're evil aliens from a far-away planet sent to make students' lives miserable... Anyway, the point is they're not your friend, so don't talk to them like one, otherwise they'll mark you down. Harshly.

The Mark Scheme

Mark Scheme — something that helps the examiner to figure out what level your exam answer is at so they can work out what mark to give it — and not the chief examiner's name. Easy mistake to make though...

Your answer will be given a **Level** from **1** to **5**

- Each level has a description of the **key features** the examiner is **looking for** in your answer.
- The examiner will try to **judge** which **level** your answer **matches best**.
- The examiner will then decide what **mark** to give you **within** that **level**. For example, if the examiner thinks that you've written a **high level 3** answer, then you might be awarded **18 marks**.
- Your **overall grade** will be **worked out later** after everyone's results have been collected.

This mark scheme is **similar** to the one the examiner uses:

Level	Description	Marks
1	Brief statements about the topic. Doesn't show clear understanding of the question. Facts are wrong. A few sentences and paragraphs. Poorly written.	1-6
2	Brief statements showing some understanding of the question being asked. Some facts are correct. Written in paragraphs, but poorly written.	7-12
3	Shows understanding of the question. Facts will mostly be correct. Events may be described rather than explained, or explained in little detail. It may not discuss points related to the question or only discuss one point without considering others. Written clearly and in paragraphs.	13-18
4	Understands the question and provides an explanation using well-structured paragraphs. Most facts will be accurate and used to support the explanation. Begins to reach conclusions. May not cover all the key points or the whole time period. Very well written.	19-24
5	Answers the question directly. The essay will acknowledge a range of factors and it will show an understanding of how factors and their relationships change over time. It will consider virtually the whole time period. Points that are made will be developed and clearly explained. Facts will be accurate and support the argument. The answer will reach a conclusion. Written and structured excellently.	25-30

Beat all the levels, rescue the princess, complete the exam.

Get to know the mark scheme. If you know what the examiner is looking for, you'll have a better idea of how to get a higher mark.

My best friends — Mark Scheme, Natalie Curriculum and Keeley Stage V

Basically, to get a good mark you need to answer the question. That sounds pretty obvious, but lots of people end up writing about what they know, and not what the question asks for. Answer the question properly and you should go far...

How to Structure Your Answer

Structuring your answer will keep you focused on the question in the exam. Knowing exactly what you are going to write will also make your answer flow much better. Exciting stuff this, and it could save your life... probably...

A **Good Introduction** shows that you **Understand** the **Question**

Your introduction sets the tone of your essay. Give the examiner a **good first impression**.

1) Identify what the **key factor** is going to be in your essay.
2) **Mention** other **factors**, **alternative arguments** or other **reasons**.
3) Show that you **know** the **significance** of the **time** and **people/events** in the question.

Don't spend **too long** on your introduction. Leave yourself **enough time** for the rest of the answer.

The **Main Paragraphs** show your **Argument**

Your paragraphs need to be **clear** and **concise** so that the examiner can easily follow your argument.

1) Try to write **5-8** paragraphs.
2) Each paragraph should make a **new point** that **adds** to your argument.
3) Show **how** the **main factors affected** the **statement** in your **question**.
4) **Balance** your answer by showing how **other factors** were **more** or **less important** — or by making points which **argue against** the statement made in the question.

A **Conclusion** should **Answer** the question

A good conclusion shows the examiner that you've come up with your **own interpretation** of the question.

1) A conclusion is your **final answer** to the question, so it should **round off** all of your points.
2) **Sum up** the points you made in your main paragraphs. You can show how **each point** was **relevant** to your answer.
3) You need to make a **judgement**, e.g.

   which **factor** was the **most important**, or which **short-term** and **long-term** factors had the **biggest impact** on an event.

Make sure you write a conclusion, even if you're running out of time. The examiner needs to see what judgement you've come to.

In conclusion — planning makes perfect...

Plan your answer properly, focusing on the question being asked. Work out what your argument is going to be, and organise it so that there's one point per paragraph. And make sure your conclusion follows on nicely — it shouldn't introduce anything new, or go against everything you've just said — it should just be a nice summary of your argument and the points you've made.

How to Structure Paragraphs

Well-structured paragraphs are a recipe for success, but you could also try: a litre of cream, six eggs, ten tablespoons of sugar, a grating of nutmeg and a spoonful of treacle. Whisk it up and drink it down hot. Mmm... success...

Paragraphs are the **Building Blocks** of your essay

A paragraph should be **constructed** in the **same way** as an **essay**:

1) Make an **introductory** point.
2) **Support** your point with **explanation** and **factual evidence**.
3) Make a **concluding** point.

Jeff had two excellent points.

Each Paragraph needs to make a Point

1) You **won't** get many marks if you just **retell** the events. Like this...

> X When .... happened in .... war broke out.

2) Instead, your opening sentence should address the question **directly**. Like this...

> ✓ The **most important reason** for the outbreak of war was .... because ....

3) Try to **link** your paragraph to the previous one so your answer flows.

Useful words for linking points

- Firstly / Secondly...
- Another...
- Consequently,
- Further...
- Of lesser importance,

Support your Points with Evidence

1) You need to **find relevant factual evidence** and **examples** to **support** the points you are making.
2) This will allow you to **develop** what you mean by giving a more **detailed explanation**.
3) It's best if you can find **two** or **three** factual **examples** to **support** each point that you make.

End your paragraphs with a Concluding Statement

1) **Sum up** the point you made in your paragraph and **weigh up** the **importance** of the factor you've been discussing.
2) **Link** the **last sentence** with what you're going to discuss in the **next paragraph**, e.g.

> This factor was important, but economic factors were more important...

Oh, what's the point of carrying on? Oooo — sample exam questions...

In a weird way, a paragraph is just like a mini essay. So your final answer will be an essay, full of mini essays... That's just confusing — forget I said anything. Let me start again. Write your paragraphs just like mini essays, and you should be fine. Much clearer.

Sample Multi-Factor Question

The most common type of question you'll encounter is the 'multi-factor' style question. This type of question will ask you to write about a number of different factors and how they have contributed to a historical event.

Multi-factor questions ask you to think about *More* than *One Factor*

1) This type of question will ask you to explain the **causes** (or sometimes the **consequences**) of a **historical event**.

2) You will need to **weigh up** the importance of the factor in the question with **other factors** you have learnt about.

3) In the conclusion you'll need to make a **judgement** as to how **important** the factor in the **question** actually is.

> **Multi-factor questions will begin with phrases like:**
>
> - How far do you agree...
> - To what extent...
> - How accurate is it to say...

Highlight the *Key Words* in the question

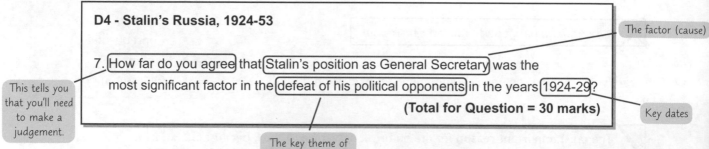

D4 - Stalin's Russia, 1924-53

7. How far do you agree that Stalin's position as General Secretary was the most significant factor in the defeat of his political opponents in the years 1924-29?

(Total for Question = 30 marks)

The factor (cause)

Key dates

This tells you that you'll need to make a judgement.

The key theme of the question

Pick out the **important bits** of the question so you can work **out** what it's asking you to do:

1) **The judgement** — e.g. 'How far do you agree'. The question is asking you to make a **judgement** on **how important** a certain factor was in **causing** a certain **event** or **consequence**.

2) **The key theme** — e.g. 'the defeat of his (Stalin's) political rivals'. The **focus** will be on how certain **factors contributed** to the **defeat** of his **political rivals**.

3) **The factor in the question** — e.g. 'Stalin's position as General Secretary'. The question will identify the **main factor**, but it's **not** the **only** factor that you should **consider**.

4) **The time period** — e.g. '1924-29'. The question focuses on the **events** in the **years 1924-29**, but **long-term** factors can **predate** these events by **months** or **years**.

The *Examiner* wants you to...

1) **Explain** the **significance** of Stalin's position as **General Secretary** in bringing about the defeat of his opponents.

2) **Compare** the **importance** of this factor with **other** possible reasons, e.g. you could mention the lack of support for his opponents.

3) Make a **judgement** as to how far you agree that Stalin's position as General Secretary was the most important factor.

4) Show how it was **more** or **less important** than any **other** factors.

How to Select the Right Information

By the time you get to the exam you'll have learnt loads of facts, but the sad thing is that you won't end up using most of them in your answers. Writing a good answer is all about selecting the right information from all the stuff in your head, and making sure it's relevant to the question. That's where these jolly pages come in.

You need to look at **Stalin**

1) The question is **focused** on **Stalin**, so you need information on him.
2) However, the information must be **relevant** to the **question**, so you should **only** use things that are **related** to **Stalin's victory** over his rivals.

The points you'd use for this are on **Page 9**

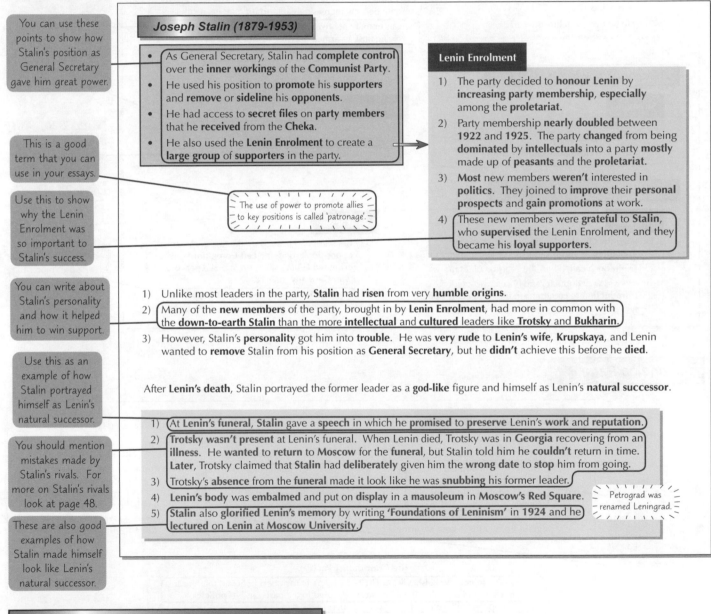

You can use these points to show how Stalin's position as General Secretary gave him great power.

Joseph Stalin (1879-1953)

*   As General Secretary, Stalin had **complete control** over the **inner workings** of the **Communist Party**.
*   He used his position to **promote** his supporters and **remove** or sideline his **opponents**.
*   He had access to **secret files** on **party members** that he **received** from the **Cheka**.
*   He also used the **Lenin Enrolment** to create a **large group** of **supporters** in the party.

This is a good term that you can use in your essays.

The use of power to promote allies to key positions is called 'patronage'.

Use this to show why the Lenin Enrolment was so important to Stalin's success.

Lenin Enrolment

1) The party decided to **honour Lenin** by **increasing party membership, especially** among the **proletariat**.
2) Party membership **nearly doubled** between **1922** and **1925**. The party **changed** from being **dominated** by **intellectuals** into a party **mostly** made up of **peasants** and the **proletariat**.
3) **Most** new members **weren't** interested in **politics**. They joined to **improve** their **personal prospects** and **gain promotions** at work.
4) These new members were **grateful** to Stalin, who **supervised** the Lenin Enrolment, and they became his **loyal supporters**.

You can write about Stalin's personality and how it helped him to win support.

1) Unlike most leaders in the party, **Stalin** had **risen** from very **humble origins**.
2) Many of the **new members** of the party, brought in by **Lenin Enrolment**, had more in common with the **down-to-earth Stalin** than the more **intellectual** and **cultured** leaders like **Trotsky** and **Bukharin**.
3) However, Stalin's **personality** got him into **trouble**. He was **very rude** to **Lenin's wife, Krupskaya**, and Lenin wanted to **remove** Stalin from his position as **General Secretary**, but he **didn't** achieve this before he **died**.

After **Lenin's death**, Stalin portrayed the former leader as a **god-like** figure and himself as Lenin's **natural successor**.

Use this as an example of how Stalin portrayed himself as Lenin's natural successor.

You should mention mistakes made by Stalin's rivals. For more on Stalin's rivals look at page 48.

These are also good examples of how Stalin made himself look like Lenin's natural successor.

1) At **Lenin's funeral, Stalin** gave a **speech** in which he **promised** to **preserve** Lenin's **work** and **reputation**.
2) **Trotsky wasn't present** at Lenin's funeral. When Lenin died, Trotsky was in **Georgia** recovering from an **illness**. He **wanted** to **return** to **Moscow** for the **funeral**, but Stalin told him he **couldn't** return in time. **Later**, Trotsky claimed that **Stalin** had **deliberately** given him the **wrong date** to **stop** him from going.
3) Trotsky's **absence** from the **funeral** made it look like he was **snubbing** his former leader.
4) **Lenin's body** was **embalmed** and put on **display** in a **mausoleum** in **Moscow's Red Square**.
5) **Stalin** also **glorified** Lenin's memory by writing **'Foundations of Leninism'** in **1924** and he **lectured** on Lenin at **Moscow University**.

Petrograd was renamed Leningrad.

There is also some useful info on **Page 10**

Stalin was prepared to be flexible with his ideology. This helped him to win more supporters.

Stalin **didn't** get **involved** in the debate on the NEP. This was a **clever** move by Stalin because it meant that he could win **support** both from those who'd **backed Bukharin** (known as 'right communists') and those who'd **backed Trotsky** (known as 'left communists').

How to Select the Right Information

You should also look at *Stalin's Rivals*

The **question** asks you about **how** Stalin **defeated** his **political opponents**, so you **need some information** on his **rivals**.

You'll find this info on *Page 7...*

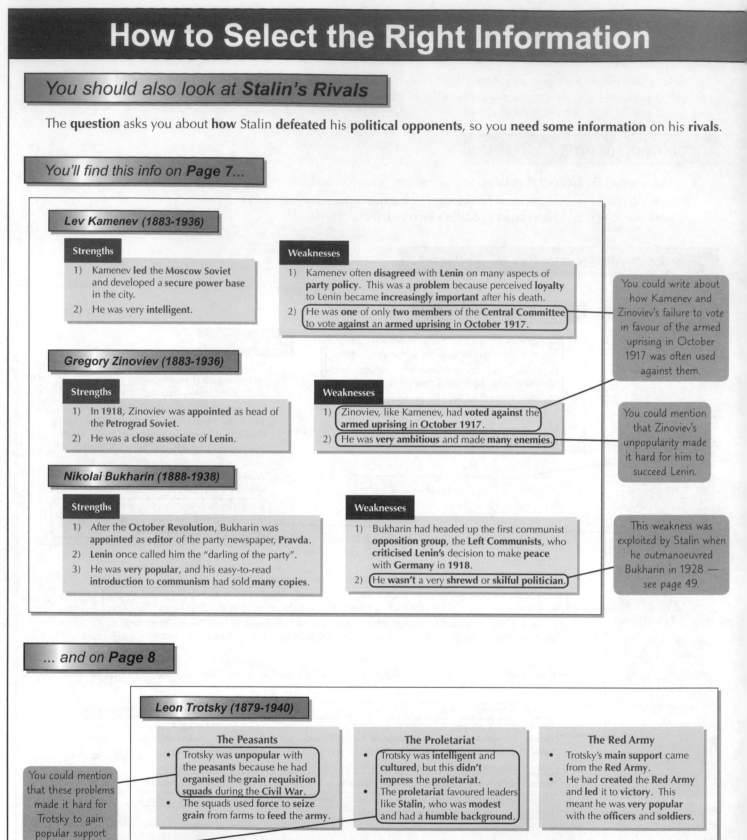

Lev Kamenev (1883-1936)

Strengths
1) Kamenev **led** the **Moscow Soviet** and developed a **secure power base** in the city.
2) He was very **intelligent**.

Weaknesses
1) Kamenev often **disagreed** with **Lenin** on many aspects of **party policy**. This was a **problem** because perceived **loyalty** to Lenin became **increasingly important** after his death.
2) He was **one** of only **two members** of the **Central Committee** to vote **against** an **armed uprising** in **October 1917**.

You could write about how Kamenev and Zinoviev's failure to vote in favour of the armed uprising in October 1917 was often used against them.

Gregory Zinoviev (1883-1936)

Strengths
1) In **1918**, Zinoviev was **appointed** as head of the **Petrograd Soviet**.
2) He was a **close associate** of **Lenin**.

Weaknesses
1) Zinoviev, like Kamenev, had **voted against** the **armed uprising** in **October 1917**.
2) He was **very ambitious** and made **many enemies**.

You could mention that Zinoviev's unpopularity made it hard for him to succeed Lenin.

Nikolai Bukharin (1888-1938)

Strengths
1) After the **October Revolution**, Bukharin was **appointed** as **editor** of the party newspaper, **Pravda**.
2) **Lenin** once called him the "darling of the party".
3) He was **very popular**, and his easy-to-read **introduction** to **communism** had sold **many copies**.

Weaknesses
1) Bukharin had headed up the first communist **opposition group**, the **Left Communists**, who **criticised** Lenin's decision to make **peace** with **Germany** in **1918**.
2) He **wasn't** a very **shrewd** or **skilful politician**.

This weakness was exploited by Stalin when he outmanoeuvred Bukharin in 1928 — see page 49.

... and on *Page 8*

Leon Trotsky (1879-1940)

The Peasants
- Trotsky was **unpopular** with the **peasants** because he had **organised** the **grain requisition squads** during the **Civil War**.
- The squads used **force** to **seize grain** from farms to **feed the army**.

The Proletariat
- Trotsky was **intelligent** and **cultured**, but this **didn't impress** the **proletariat**.
- The **proletariat** favoured leaders like **Stalin**, who was **modest** and had a **humble background**.

The Red Army
- Trotsky's **main support** came from the **Red Army**.
- He had **created** the **Red Army** and **led** it to **victory**. This meant he was **very popular** with the **officers** and **soldiers**.

You could mention that these problems made it hard for Trotsky to gain popular support against Stalin.

The Communist Party
- Trotsky only **joined** the **Bolsheviks** in **1917**. Many party members believed that because of his **background** as a **Menshevik** he **wasn't devoted** to the **party** and its **policies**.
- He was **popular** with **young** and **radical** members of the party.
- He **wasn't** a **politician** by **instinct**. He **never** tried to gain **loyal supporters** in the **party**.
- Party members **feared** Trotsky would **use** his **popularity** with the **Red Army** to set himself up as a **military dictator**, as **Napoleon Bonaparte** had done **after** the **French Revolution**.

These are good points that you could use to explain why Trotsky failed to win support in the party. They helped Stalin to defeat him.

Trotsky's past membership of the Mensheviks meant he wasn't as trusted by many Bolsheviks.

How to Select the Right Information

You need to look at *How* Stalin *Defeated* his *Opponents*

Look at the events that led to **Stalin's victory**. Try to use the **relevant information** to **decide** whether Stalin's position as **General Secretary** was the most important factor in his success or whether **other factors** were more important.

You'll find this info on **Page 12**...

This was important for Stalin because it meant he kept the power he had as General Secretary.

Make sure you show how the Triumvirate isolated Trotsky. They exploited Trotsky's weakness — see page 48. This contributed to Stalin's victory.

You can mention this as being an important victory for Stalin.

Stalin again used his power as General Secretary to undermine his rivals. Kamenev and Zinoviev lost their support bases too.

This shows Stalin using his role as General Secretary to finish off Kamenev, Zinoviev and Trotsky's struggle for the leadership.

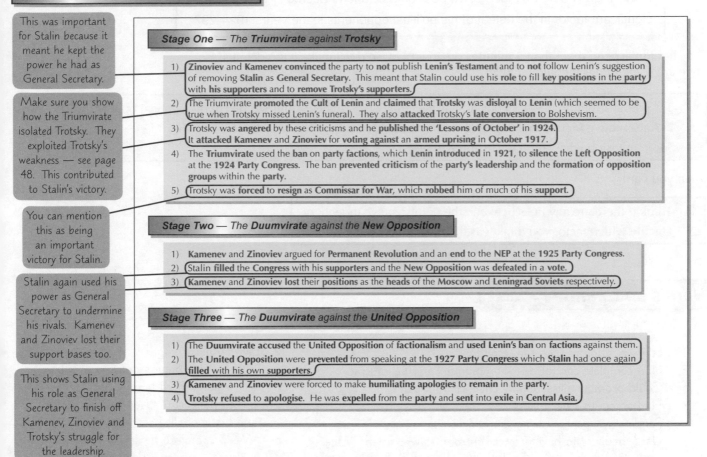

Stage One — The *Triumvirate* against *Trotsky*

1) **Zinoviev** and **Kamenev** convinced the party to **not publish Lenin's Testament** and to **not** follow Lenin's suggestion of removing **Stalin** as **General Secretary**. This meant that Stalin could use his **role** to fill **key positions** in the **party** with **his supporters** and to **remove Trotsky's supporters**.

2) The Triumvirate **promoted** the **Cult of Lenin** and **claimed** that **Trotsky** was **disloyal** to **Lenin** (which seemed to be true when Trotsky missed Lenin's funeral). They also **attacked** Trotsky's **late conversion** to Bolshevism.

3) Trotsky was **angered** by these criticisms and he **published** the **'Lessons of October'** in **1924**. It **attacked Kamenev** and **Zinoviev** for **voting against** an **armed uprising** in **October 1917**.

4) The **Triumvirate** used the **ban** on **party factions**, which **Lenin introduced** in 1921, to **silence** the **Left Opposition** at the **1924 Party Congress**. The ban **prevented criticism** of the **party's leadership** and the **formation** of **opposition groups** within the party.

5) Trotsky was **forced** to **resign** as **Commissar for War**, which **robbed** him of much of his **support**.

Stage Two — The *Duumvirate* against the *New Opposition*

1) **Kamenev** and **Zinoviev** argued for **Permanent Revolution** and an **end** to the **NEP** at the **1925 Party Congress**.

2) **Stalin filled** the **Congress** with his **supporters** and the **New Opposition** was **defeated** in a **vote**.

3) **Kamenev** and **Zinoviev** lost their **positions** as the **heads** of the **Moscow** and **Leningrad Soviets** respectively.

Stage Three — The *Duumvirate* against the *United Opposition*

1) The **Duumvirate** accused the **United Opposition** of **factionalism** and **used Lenin's ban** on **factions** against them.

2) The **United Opposition** were **prevented** from speaking at the **1927 Party Congress** which **Stalin** had once again **filled** with his own **supporters**.

3) **Kamenev** and **Zinoviev** were forced to make **humiliating apologies** to **remain** in the **party**.

4) **Trotsky refused** to **apologise**. He was **expelled** from the **party** and **sent** into **exile** in **Central Asia**.

... *and on* **Page 13**

This is another example you could mention that shows Stalin's ideological flexibility. It helped him to gain a lot of support.

You can use this point to show how Stalin exploited Bukharin's weaknesses.

This is a good detail you can add to your essays.

It's important to remember that Trotsky wasn't just defeated by Stalin.

Stage Four — Stalin against the *Right Opposition*

1) In **1927-28** a **rumour** spread around the USSR that the **foreign powers** were about to **launch an attack**. The **peasants** began to **hoard** their **grain**, which led to **food shortages** in the **towns** and **cities**. The **rumours** were **false**, and the **NEP** was **blamed** for the crisis because it **didn't** allow for **state control** of the **peasants**.

2) Even though the **NEP** was **unpopular** within the party, **Bukharin** remained a **strong supporter** of it.

3) But in **1928**, **Stalin** stunned Bukharin by proposing to **end the NEP** immediately and **implement** a policy of **collectivisation** of **agriculture** and **rapid industrialisation** through a **Five-Year Plan** (see page 15).

4) Stalin's economic policies were **almost identical** to Trotsky's, so the **leaderless Left Communists** supported Stalin. Furthermore, Stalin **appealed** to the **majority** of **communists** who **hated** the **NEP**.

5) **Bukharin** was **popular**, but he **wasn't** as **shrewd** as **Stalin** and he was **outmanoeuvred**. **Bukharin** was **removed** from the **party leadership** and Stalin was left to **become** the new **vozhd** (boss) of the **USSR**.

- Stalin's enemies **seriously underestimated** him — they called him 'Comrade Card Index' because they thought he was **just an administrator**. However, **Stalin** used his **administrative role** to gain a **huge amount** of **power**.

- **Trotsky** became **isolated** after Lenin's death and he had **many enemies**. The **Triumvirate** formed to **defeat** Trotsky, and when he tried to **fight back** they used their combined **power** and **influence** to undermine him.

- Trotsky took decisions that made it seem he was **strangely reluctant** to **become** the next leader. In **1922**, **Lenin** offered him the role of **Deputy Chairman of Sovnarkom** (a body like a cabinet of ministers) — a position that would have strengthened his chance of becoming Lenin's **successor**. But he **refused**.

How to Plan Your Answer

This page will help you plan for a multi-factor type question, like the one on page 46.

Use a **Plan** to **Structure** your **Argument**

Here's the question again:

> How far do you agree that Stalin's position as General Secretary was the most significant factor in the defeat of his political opponents in the years 1924-29?

You shouldn't spend more than **5 minutes** on your plan, so don't make it too detailed. Here are some things it could include:

1) **3-4 points** about how Stalin's position as General Secretary helped him to defeat his political opponents.
2) **2-3 alternative factors** that might have contributed to Stalin's victory (with **reasons why**).
3) Some notes on what your **conclusion** will be.

Then you can:

1) Think if there are any **links** between the points you've thought of.
2) **Decide** which factor you think was the **most important**.

Here's an **Example Plan**

Your plan probably won't be as big as this. We've written it in full so it's easier to follow.

1. Stalin's position as General Secretary
   - Had complete control over Communist Party bureaucracy.
   - Could promote allies, remove enemies from party.
   - Had access to Cheka files.
   - Personally supervised Lenin Enrolment.
   - Used influence to have greater control over who attended the Party Congress. He could fill the Congress with his supporters.

2. Stalin's other strengths
   - Had humble origins, ordinary members of the party loved him.
   - Skilled politician. Used Cult of Lenin and tactic of alliances well.
   - Was prepared to be flexible with his policies — e.g. over the NEP.

3. Weaknesses of political opponents
   - Kamenev and Zinoviev had voted against the armed uprising in 1917.
   - Bukharin wasn't a skilled politician and lacked a power base.
   - Trotsky was unpopular and strangely reluctant to take power.

Defeating Stalin's political opponents

4. Mistakes of political opponents
   - All the opponents underestimated Stalin.
   - Trotsky allowed himself to become isolated — his 'Lessons of October' provoked Kamenev and Zinoviev to attack him.
   - The opponents didn't work together to defeat Stalin — instead they made alliances with him.

5. Stalin's victory — conclusion
   - Position as General Secretary was the most significant factor because it helped him to win key votes and it helped him to control the party.
   - He could also capitalise on the weaknesses and mistakes of his opponents.
   - Other strengths were important, but they were mainly used in his role as General Secretary.
   - Control over the Party Congress was also very significant. It allowed Stalin to have some control over the party's policies and decisions.

Worked Answer

These pages will show you how to take an okay answer and turn it into a really good one that will impress the examiner.

Use your **Introduction** to get off to a **Good Start**

These pages are all about how to word your sentences to impress the examiner, so we haven't included everything from the plan on page 50.

You might start with something like...

> Stalin managed to defeat Kamenev, Zinoviev, Bukharin and Trotsky. His position as General Secretary was significant in his victory, but there were other significant factors as well.

This intro is **okay** because it...
1) **Gives** the **names** of Stalin's **political opponents**.
2) Identifies the **main factor** in the **question**.
3) Suggests that **other factors** were involved.

However, it **doesn't** say what the **significance** of **Stalin's position** as **General Secretary** was. For example:

> In the years 1924-29 Stalin was able to defeat his political opponents to become the leader of the USSR. As General Secretary of the party, Stalin was in a (very strong position) to create a powerful support base. He used his position to pack the party conferences with his supporters and this meant he won all the important votes.

This shows how significant you think his position was.

You could finish by showing that you're going to talk about **other factors** as well:

> But there were other important factors in Stalin's victory. (Stalin had the political skill) to use his strong position. He manipulated his opponents by using the tactic of making and breaking alliances to undermine his political rivals. Kamenev, Zinoviev, Bukharin and Trotsky also contributed to their own downfall by (underestimating Stalin's strength, failing to build up their own power bases and through their own errors of judgement.)

You've identified several other factors here.

You've identified Stalin's political skill as a factor.

Make your **First Paragraph** about the **Key Factor**

> Stalin's position as General Secretary was very significant in helping him to overcome his political opponents. Stalin used the support he gained from Lenin Enrolment to challenge his rivals at the Party Congress. At the 1925 Party Congress, Kamenev and Zinoviev attempted to introduce Permanent Revolution as party policy. This was defeated in a vote, and at the 1927 Party Congress the United Opposition was silenced.

Good use of examples.

1) This paragraph **shows** the **powerful position** of Stalin and gives some **good examples**.
2) But it **doesn't** explain the **connection** between the **position** of **General Secretary** and **Stalin's ability** to **manipulate** the **Communist Party**.
3) To **improve** the paragraph you could **focus** on the question **more directly**:

> As General Secretary, Stalin was in charge of the Communist Party's bureaucracy. This gave him great influence over party policy, and also gave him access to the Cheka's secret files on other party members. Stalin had the power to promote his supporters and sideline his enemies. Stalin's position also allowed him to personally supervise the Lenin Enrolment, which meant that many of the new party members owed their membership to Stalin. This greatly increased Stalin's personal support in the party, and this popularity meant that he had many supporters in the Party Congress. (He used this support to defeat his opponents in important votes.)

This explains how Stalin's position gave him so much influence.

Good example of how Stalin used his power.

Worked Answer

You need to write about Other Factors

You might start like this:

> There were also other factors that were significant in allowing Stalin to defeat his rivals. His political opponents had weaknesses of their own, and they made mistakes which damaged their ability to challenge him.

Using this word links your point back to the question.

1) This paragraph introduces **other factors** that **led** to the **defeat** of **Stalin's opponents**.

2) However, you can make this paragraph **better** by including **examples** of these **weaknesses**:

Good examples of mistakes made by Stalin's rivals.

> Stalin's opponents did not always help themselves. Trotsky lost popular support by failing to attend Lenin's funeral, and his attack on Kamenev and Zinoviev in his 'Lessons of October' backfired. This meant Trotsky became even more isolated. But the biggest failing of all of Stalin's rivals was that they underestimated how powerful Stalin was. They referred to him as 'Comrade Card Index' and they saw him as just an administrator.

This paragraph is **good** because it provides some examples of **other factors**, but you can **develop** this point by showing how these weaknesses benefited Stalin:

Here you're showing that you're answering the question.

> Trotsky was Stalin's biggest rival to succeed Lenin. The weakening and isolation of Trotsky significantly helped Stalin in the struggle to succeed Lenin. Trotsky's unpopularity meant that in 1925 he was forced to resign as Commissar for War, which made him even weaker. Furthermore, Stalin's rivals were so focused on fighting each other that they didn't challenge Stalin until it was too late. Stalin's influence and popularity in the party made him far more powerful than his rivals, but they didn't realise this.

You could Show how Different Factors are Linked Together

You could say:

This is another good factor to mention.
Good examples of tactics used by Stalin.
Good use of historical vocab.

> Stalin was a very skilful politician. He promoted the Cult of Lenin and by doing this he promoted himself. By speaking at Lenin's funeral and writing and lecturing about the former leader, Stalin made himself appear to be Lenin's natural successor. Moreover, Stalin was able to use a tactic of making and breaking alliances with his opponents to isolate his rivals and pick them off. The success of the Triumvirate and the Duumvirate were crucial in helping Stalin to succeed Lenin.

1) This paragraph **introduces** a **new factor** and gives some **good examples** of why it was **important** in helping Stalin defeat his political opponents.

2) However, you could **link** the **other factors** to the **key factor**:

> However, Stalin's skill as a politician was only important because he was General Secretary. For example, Stalin was able to create the Cult of Lenin because, as General Secretary, he was important enough to give a speech at Lenin's funeral and able to glorify Lenin's memory by writing and lecturing about him. Furthermore, Stalin's important and powerful position meant that Zinoviev, Kamenev and Bukharin all wanted to make alliances with him.

Here you've stated that while other factors are important — they all link to Stalin's position as General Secretary.

Here you're explaining how Stalin's position as General Secretary helped him to use his political skill.

This shows that while **Stalin's skill** as a **politician** was an **important factor** in helping him to defeat his rivals, it was **because** Stalin was **General Secretary** that he was **able** to **use** his **skill successfully**.

Worked Answer

Finish *your essay in* Style

Your conclusion should **refer back** to the **key points** that you've made in each paragraph.
If you've linked your paragraphs well then you'll have **created an argument**.

You could start with something like this:

> Stalin's position as General Secretary was (very significant) in defeating his
> political opponents between 1924 and 1929. He was able to use this position
> to increase his own support and gain the loyalty of the ordinary working
> members of the party. He then used this support to defeat his opponents.

This shows that you're considering the question.

This is **okay**, but you can then **create balance** by referring to **other factors**. Like this:

> Other factors played a role in Stalin's victory. Stalin's own political skill enabled him
> to manipulate his opponents with (remarkable ease.) His rivals could not overcome
> their own weaknesses to pose a serious threat to Stalin's dominance.

Here you're making a judgement about the strength of Stalin's political skill.

This is better because it shows you've **considered** other factors in your conclusion.

You need to make a Judgement

You **won't** have **answered** the question until you've made a **judgement** on which factor you think was **most important**.

You could write your judgement like this:

This links back to the question and everything else you've written.

> Stalin's position as (General Secretary was very significant,) but it was a
> combination of factors, including Stalin's strengths and his opponents'
> weaknesses, which allowed him to take power in the USSR.

1) This kind of judgement is **fine**. It shows that you think **all** the **factors**
   were of **similar importance** in Stalin's defeat of his political opponents.

2) But, you can write a more **forceful** conclusion like this:

> However, although there were other important factors that contributed to Stalin's
> success, it was his position as General Secretary that allowed him to manipulate the
> situation following Lenin's death to his own advantage. Lenin wrote in his Testament
> that, as General Secretary, Stalin had "unlimited authority concentrated in his hands".
> Ultimately this was the most significant factor in enabling him to defeat his opponents.

This is a good justification of your choice.

This kind of in-depth knowledge will really impress the examiner.

Picking one factor over others shows that you've thought about your decision.

This judgement is **better** because you've shown the examiner that, after considering **all** the factors,
you've reached a decision on which factor was the **most important**. You've also **justified** this choice.

It doesn't matter which factor you choose — just make sure that you make a **judgement** and **justify** why you've made it.

Sample Single-Factor Question

Another type of question you might come across in the exam is the single-factor question. As you might have guessed, these questions will ask you to write about one factor or one historical event.

Make sure you *Stick* to the *Point*

1) This type of question is asking whether you **agree** or **disagree** with a statement, or whether something has **changed** or **developed** over time.

2) You might also have to make a **judgement** about an individual, action, policy or idea.

> **Single-factor questions will begin with phrases like:**
> - How successful was...
> - Do you agree that...
> - How significant was...
> - To what extent...

1) A single factor question may ask you about the **importance** of a **single** event, factor or individual. So you can either:
   - Write about the ways in which the **single factor** was **significant** or **not significant**, or...
   - Write about how the **single factor** was **significant** and suggest **other** more **significant factors**.

2) Or it will ask you whether a **single factor** has **changed over time**. So you should:
   - Write about the ways in which the **single factor changed**, and...
   - Write about the ways in which the **single factor stayed the same**.

Highlight the *Key Words* in the question

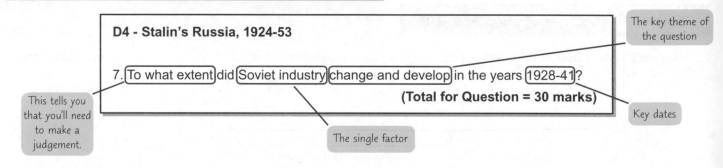

D4 - Stalin's Russia, 1924-53

7. To what extent did Soviet industry change and develop in the years 1928-41?

(Total for Question = 30 marks)

The key theme of the question

This tells you that you'll need to make a judgement.

The single factor

Key dates

Pick out the **important bits** of the question so you can work out what it's asking you to do:

1) **The judgement** — e.g. 'To what extent'. The question is asking you to make a **judgement** as to how far this **single factor changed** or **stayed the same** over a **period of time**.

2) **The single factor** — e.g. 'Soviet industry'. This is the **only** factor you need to **consider**.

3) **The key theme** — e.g. 'change and develop'. The **focus** of your answer will be on how the **single factor**, Soviet industry, **changed**, **developed** or **stayed the same**.

4) **The time period** — e.g. '1928-41'. The question gives you a **long** time period to **find evidence** from, so **don't** look at anything **before** or **after** these dates.

The *Examiner* wants you to...

1) **Identify** the **developments** in **Soviet industry** during the period **1928-41**. This time period begins with the end of the NEP and runs to the beginning of war with Germany. It includes the first three Five-Year Plans.

2) **Consider** the **extent** to which Soviet industry had **changed**, **developed** and/or **stayed the same** during these years.

3) Make a **judgement** as to the **extent** of **change** and **development** throughout the years **1928-41**.

How to Select the Right Information

Here's another set of lovely pages which show you how to select the relevant information from this book for the exam.

Select the Information that's Relevant to the Question

You need to think about the state of Soviet industry **before** the **plans** were **introduced** — and what the plans' **aims** and **achievements** were.

You'll find this info on **Page 15**...

You can mention what Stalin was trying to achieve and why he wanted to do it so quickly.

The period **1928-1941** has been called the **second communist revolution** because it saw **major changes**. In **1931** Stalin gave a **speech** in which he stated that the **USSR** was "**fifty** to a **hundred years behind** the **advanced** [western] **countries**". He warned that they needed to "**close** the **gap within ten years**" or the USSR would be "**crushed**".

You should mention that Stalin wanted to rapidly industrialise the USSR because he also wanted to change Soviet society.

Plans for Industry

- **Five-Year Plans** would be introduced to **industrialise** the country at **great speed**.
- These would **increase** the numbers of the **proletariat**, the **traditional supporters** of the **Communist Party**.
- The USSR's **industry** would provide **improved technology** that would make **farming** more **efficient**.

... and on **Page 18**

1) The **Communist Party** was traditionally the **party** of the proletariat. Stalin hoped that the **expansion** of **industry** would **increase** the **size** of the **proletariat** and therefore create **more** loyal party members.

2) The USSR was the **only** communist state in the world. Stalin was **convinced** that its enemies would try to destroy it. He felt that only an **economically** and **militarily strong USSR** could defend itself.

You can point out that in 1928 Soviet industry was growing slowly. Stalin wanted to change this.

3) The **NEP** was **becoming** increasingly **unpopular**. Many **new** party members, who were recruited during the **Lenin Enrolment** (see page 9), believed that it **wasn't** helping to **create** an **equal society** because it had **encouraged** the **growth** of the **Nepmen** (urban traders who benefited from the NEP) in the **towns** and the **kulaks** in the **countryside**.

4) The **NEP** had been **successful** in helping the **economy** to **recover** after the **Civil War**, but by **1928 economic progress** was **slowing** and the NEP **wasn't delivering** the industrialisation the USSR **needed**.

You could mention that these were the main industries that the first Five-Year Plan was aimed at improving.

1) The **first plan** was aimed at developing **heavy industries**, such as **coal**, **iron**, **steel**, **oil** and **heavy machinery**. Stalin believed these were the **building blocks** of an **advanced industrial economy**.

2) **New industrial plants** were built to the **east** of the **Ural Mountains** where they would be **safe** if the USSR was **invaded** from the **west**. Uzbekistan and Kazakhstan were **developed economically** for the **first time**.

These are examples that you can use of how Soviet industry was changing during the first Five-Year Plan.

3) **New cities** were built from **scratch**. The **most** important was **Magnitogorsk**, which went from being a **small village** in **1928** to a **town** of **250 000** people in **1932**. However, the people **lived** and **worked** in **terrible conditions**.

4) **Electricity** was **vital** to the **first plan** — the **massive hydroelectric Dnieprostroi Dam** was built on the **River Dnieper**.

5) **Tractor factories** were built in **Stalingrad** and **car factories** in **Moscow**. **Canals**, built by prisoners, **connected Moscow** with the **River Volga**, and **Leningrad** with the **White Sea**.

How to Select the Right Information

Try to use some Facts and Figures to support your Arguments

Try to remember some of the **important statistics** from the Five-Year Plans to **strengthen** the points you make in your essay.

You'll find this info on Page 19...

You can use these figures to support an argument about the growth in output of certain industries.

	1928 Output	1932 Output	1932 Target Output
Electricity (billion kWh)	5.05	13.4	17.0
Coal (million tonnes)	35.4	64.3	68.0
Oil (million tonnes)	11.7	21.4	19.0
Pig-iron (million tonnes)	3.3	6.2	8.0
Steel (million tonnes)	4.0	5.9	8.3

You can use this to balance a point about a growth in output.

Although **oil** was the **only** industry to **exceed** its **target**, the general **increase** in **output** during the **first** Five-Year Plan was very **impressive**. However, the **unrealistic targets** that were set meant that **managers** were more **concerned** about the **quantity** of what they produced, rather than the **quality**.

The Second Five-Year Plan — January 1933 to December 1937

You can write about the changes in different industries.

1) To **improve** the **agricultural output** from **collectivisation**, more **mechanical agricultural equipment**, such as **tractors** and **combine harvesters**, were built.

2) **Railways** and **canals** were built **between** the **new centres** of **industry** to ease the transport of goods and raw materials.

This is an example of something that didn't improve in this period.

3) There were **some attempts** to **increase** the **supply** of **consumer goods**, but they **remained** a **low priority** for Stalin. New **boots** and **shoes** became **nearly impossible** to obtain.

4) **Stalin** was interested in building 'showpiece' developments for **propaganda purposes**. The **Moscow Metro**, with its **chandeliers** and **marble statues** of **heroic workers**, was built during the second plan.

5) The **new factories** built during the **first plan** became **fully functioning** during the **second plan**. These **contributed** to the **second plan's success** as they greatly **increased** output in these years.

You could consider how methods were changed to increase productivity.

6) A **system** of **wages** was **introduced** which **rewarded** those who made **greater efforts** than others.

... and on Page 20

The Stakhanovite Movement

- In **1935**, it was reported that a **miner** from the **Donbass region**, **Alexei Stakhanov**, had mined **102 tonnes** of **coal** in a **six-hour shift**. This was **fourteen times** his **allotted quota**.

- Soon after, it was reported he'd **broken** his record by mining **227 tonnes**.

You could mention that incentives were developed to increase productivity.

- He received many awards, and the **Stakhanovite movement** was **created** to **reward workers** who **exceeded** their **quotas**.

- In **1988**, a Soviet newspaper **revealed** his **achievements** were **massively exaggerated**.

Try to remember some key facts that you can use as evidence to support your arguments.

	1932 Output	1937 Output	1937 Target Output
Electricity (billion kWh)	13.4	36.7	38.0
Coal (million tonnes)	64.3	128.0	152.0
Oil (million tonnes)	21.4	28.5	46.8
Pig-iron (million tonnes)	6.2	14.5	16.0
Steel (million tonnes)	5.9	17.7	17.0

Some industries fell **well short** of their **target output level**. But despite this, the **figures** still **show** that in the major industries output **significantly increased** in this period.

SECTION 6 — WRITING YOUR ANSWER

How to Select the Right Information

You need to remember information for the **Whole Period**

You've got to provide evidence for the **whole period**, so make sure you look at the third Five-Year Plan too. Also try to think of examples of where Soviet industry didn't change in this period.

You'll find this info on **Page 20**...

> The shift in Stalin's priorities for Soviet industry was an important change that you can mention.

> You could look at reasons why the Five-Year Plans weren't as successful as they could have been, e.g. the purges.

Priorities changed during the course of the **third plan**, as **war** with Nazi Germany **seemed increasingly likely**.

1) The third plan began with a **focus** on producing **consumer goods**, such as **radios** and **cars**.
2) However, Stalin feared that **war** would **break out** between the **USSR** and **Nazi Germany**. Consequently, the third plan became **increasingly** devoted to the **production** of **aircraft**, **tanks** and **weapons**. By **1940**, a **third** of the **government's budget** was **spent** on the **USSR's military**.
3) The Nazi **invasion** in **June 1941** meant that the **third plan** only lasted **three** and a **half years**.
4) During the third plan, **output** grew **very little** in many industries. This was partly due to Stalin's **purges** (see pages 27-29), which led to the **imprisonment** or **execution** of many **skilled workers**.
5) **Internal passports** were created to **control** the **movement** of **people** in the USSR. This **stopped** workers from **regularly changing** their **jobs** and **ensured** that **factories** had a **stable workforce**.

... and on **Page 21**

> You could mention that despite some success for Soviet industry there were also some failures.

> This is good evidence for the success of the changes to Soviet industry.

Economy and Industry

1) Between **1928** and **1940**, the **USSR** was **transformed** from a largely **agricultural country** into one of the **leading industrial powers** in Europe. However, **production** was still very **inefficient**.
2) The **1930s** was the **decade** of the **Great Depression** and most countries suffered **falling production** and **high unemployment**. The **USSR** experienced the **opposite** of this. The **success** of the Five-Year Plans was a great **propaganda triumph** for the Communist Party.
3) **Major projects** such as **Magnitogorsk** and the **Moscow Metro** impressed **Soviets** and **foreigners** alike.
4) Stalin worried that without **rapid** industrialisation the **USSR** would be "**crushed**". However, in the **Second World War** the **USSR** had the **industrial power** to **defeat** the **Nazis**. This seemed to **prove** Stalin was **right**.

> You can give examples of things that stayed the same for the Soviets.

> You can mention how the changes in Soviet industry had a major impact on the people.

> You could say that some changes were good for Soviet workers.

USSR's Society

1) In the period **1928-1941 life** was still **tough** for **most people** in the **USSR**. **Wages weren't high** and there were **few consumer goods** available in the shops.
2) The **population** of **towns** and **cities** more than **doubled** between **1928** and **1941** as **peasants flocked** to **towns** to find **work** in **industry**. Furthermore, by **1940 women** accounted for **40%** of the **labour force**.
3) Many Soviets, especially **young people**, were prepared to **work very hard** to make the **plans succeed**. They were **convinced** by Stalin's **propaganda** that they could **achieve** the **seemingly impossible**.
4) This period saw **more investment** in **health care** and **education**. The number of **doctors** in the USSR **nearly trebled** and **everyone** was **entitled** to **free medical assistance**. **Illiteracy** was **greatly reduced** and **more people** went to **university**. **Paid holidays** were also introduced.

How to Plan Your Answer

This page will help you plan for a single-factor type question, like the one on page 54.

Use a *Plan* to *Structure* your *Argument*

Here's the question again:

> To what extent did Soviet industry change and develop in the years 1928-41?

You're going to have to find a way of **sorting** all the **evidence** into an answer that makes a **point**. You've not got long, so keep your plan **brief**. Here are some things it could include:

1) Evidence of **change over time**.
2) Notes on aspects of Soviet industry that **changed**, **developed** or **stayed the same**.
3) Some notes on your **conclusion**.

Link your paragraphs *together*

1) This question is specifically asking you about the **single-factor** in the question **changed over time**.
2) To show **how** the single-factor **changed over time** you could begin by looking at the single-factor at the **start** of the **time period** in the question. You could then write about the **ways** in which the **single-factor changed** (e.g. for this question, by looking at how **Soviet industry grew** and how it **developed** between **1928** and **1941**). You could then write about the **ways** in which the single-factor **stayed the same** over the time period.
3) Select **relevant supporting material** for each point.

Here's an *Example Plan*

Your plan probably won't be as big as this. We've written it in full so it's easier to follow.

1. The state of Soviet industry in 1928
- NEP was still being used.
- Soviet industry was still at a small scale.
- Soviet industry was growing slowly.

5. Conclusions
- A massive increase in the scale of Soviet industry — meant the USSR could survive the Nazi invasion.
- Nature of Soviet industry evolved as priorities changed.
- However, several things remained the same — so the change wasn't so great in certain areas.

Change and development in Soviet Industry

2. How Soviet industry grew in 1928-41
- Heavy industry grew rapidly.
- Output of many important raw materials grew significantly (use figures for this).
- More and more people left the countryside to work in factories — the proletariat grew.
- Large-scale projects like Magnitogorsk and the hydroelectric dam at Dnieprostroi were developed to transform Soviet industry.

4. Aspects of Soviet industry that stayed the same
- Poor working conditions for the workers.
- A continued emphasis on heavy industry.
- Consumer industry continued to be sidelined.

3. How Soviet industry developed in 1928-41
- The aims of the Five-Year Plans changed.
- The first plan — focused on improving the USSR's heavy industry and increasing the extraction of raw materials, electricity production and machinery production.
- The second plan — aimed at developing Soviet industry to boost agricultural production, as well as improving transport links to assist the growth of Soviet industry.
- The third plan — priorities for Soviet industry changed from strengthening the consumer industry to arming the USSR.

Worked Answer

These pages will take an ordinary, everyday, uninspiring answer and turn it into pure exam gold. Oooooooh shiny...

Use your **Introduction** to get the examiner's **Attention**

You could write something like this...

> In 1928 Soviet industry was backward and inefficient — Stalin was determined that Soviet industry should be modernised. Stalin also wanted to develop Soviet industry to create a larger and stronger proletariat in the USSR. Between 1928 and 1941 he introduced three Five-Year Plans to achieve this. By 1941 Soviet industry had undergone major development and the USSR was able to defeat Nazi Germany in the Second World War.

Good use of historical vocab.

This intro is **okay** because it shows that Soviet industry **changed over time**, but it **doesn't**...

1) Say **how** industry changed over time.
2) Give a **balanced response**.

To make the introduction **better** you could make more **specific references** to what happened in **1928-41**:

> During the years 1928-41 Soviet industry underwent a major transformation. In 1928 Soviet industry was relatively small-scale and it was only growing slowly. However, by 1941 it was on a far larger scale and some key industries had grown significantly. This was achieved through the use of three Five-Year Plans which developed and changed over time. However, the changes didn't benefit all types of industry — in 1941 Soviet industry was still based on heavy industry, with little production of consumer goods.

Here you've shown change over time.

Here you've balanced your introduction by showing that there is evidence of continuity over time.

This introduction is **quite similar**, but it refers **more directly** to the **change** in the period and it is **more balanced**.

Make sure you **Don't** just **Retell** the **Story**

You might start your next paragraph with:

> In 1928 Stalin introduced the first Five-Year Plan. It was designed to build up heavy industry by increasing the production of coal, oil, steel and machinery. Stalin also started shifting the USSR's industry to new, large industrial towns located in the east of the country, away from the USSR's enemies. The first Five-Year Plan was quite successful in increasing production, but the quality of the products was often poor and the targets were very difficult to achieve.

1) This paragraph is **fine**, but you've only got about **30 minutes** to answer the question and you'll **run out of time** if you **describe** each plan in **great detail**.
2) You'll get more marks if you **organise** your **paragraphs**. For example, you could write about the **changes** that happened, **developments** which occurred and things that **stayed** the **same**.
3) So, you could **begin** by looking at the **changes** that happened, like this:

> In the years 1928-41 Soviet industry transformed quite considerably. The more mixed economy of the New Economic Policy was replaced by a command economy based on targets. Soviet industry was transformed by projects such as those at Magnitogorsk and by the hydroelectric dam built at Dnieprostroi. These projects helped industry to grow at an impressive rate. Production in raw materials and heavy industrial products rose greatly, for example, between 1928 and 1937 coal and steel output approximately quadrupled.

Here you've shown that you're addressing the question.

This is a reference to something that has changed during the time period.

Good example of how changes to Soviet industry helped to increase output.

Good examples of the change in the scale of Soviet industry.

Worked Answer

Consider the **Whole Period** in the question

You need to make sure you assess how **Soviet industry developed over time**. You could write...

Here you're showing that the focus of Soviet industry developed over time.

> The nature of the Five-Year Plans developed between 1928 and 1941 as Stalin's priorities changed. This meant that the first Five-Year Plan was quite different from the second.

This paragraph is **okay** and it introduces the idea that Soviet industry **developed over time**. However, it is quite **vague** and it **doesn't provide** any **examples**. You could improve it like this...

These are good examples of how the focus of industry changed.

> The nature of the Five-Year Plans developed over time. The first plan was focused on building up the USSR's heavy industry and increasing electricity and machinery production. However, it become clear that many of the targets set by Gosplan were unachievable. The second plan had more realistic targets and it focused on developing the USSR's transport network to help boost industrial output.

You can **add** to this point by looking at the third Five-Year Plan:

Good example of an external factor that influenced the development of Soviet industry.

> During the 1930s the international situation became more tense and Nazi Germany posed a serious threat to the USSR. Consequently, the drive to increase consumer production in the third Five-Year Plan was replaced by the necessity to increase military production.

Good linking word.

Here you've shown what change there was in Soviet industry.

Don't forget to mention ways in which **Soviet Industry Didn't Change**

You should show **awareness** that some aspects of Soviet industry **stayed the same**:

> Output in several industries increased and Soviet industry developed greatly at this time, but some industries remained stagnant and the living conditions of many Soviets changed very little.

Here you've provided examples of some things that stayed the same.

This is **good** because you've introduced some **examples** of ways in which Soviet industry **didn't change**. But you need to provide some **evidence** to **support** your **examples**:

> Soviet industry remained focused on developing the USSR's heavy industry and the extraction of raw materials. This meant few consumer goods were produced and many Soviets could not buy things like new shoes or boots. Furthermore, Soviet workers continued to live and work in terrible conditions, which were especially bad in new industrial centres like Magnitogorsk.

Here you've provided evidence to support your examples.

This paragraph is **better**, but you could **improve** it further by **linking** it to **other factors**:

> The continued repression of the workers had a negative effect on Soviet industry. The imprisonment and execution of many highly skilled workers during the 'Great Terror' caused a slowdown in the growth of many Soviet industries.

Here you've pointed out that continued repression caused problems for Soviet industry.

Worked Answer

Make your conclusion **Balanced**

You could start with...

> Soviet heavy industry grew rapidly through the period 1928-1941 and there was a great increase in the output of machinery and raw materials. This success was achieved by three different Five-Year Plans, but the focus of these plans developed as Stalin's priorities changed. This meant that, for example, the third Five-Year Plan became focused on rearmament because of the rise of Nazi Germany.

Make sure you refer to the Five-Year Plans in this way or later on as 'the plans' or 'the first plan' — don't abbreviate to 'FYPs'.

This paragraph shows that Soviet industry **changed** and **developed** greatly during this period.

You could then add...

> However, some features of Soviet industry didn't change at all. Between 1928 and 1941 there was a continued focus on the development of the USSR's heavy industry, which meant that the consumer goods industry was largely ignored. Furthermore, not everything got better — Soviet workers continued to operate in harsh conditions and Stalin's purges slowed the growth in output.

Giving balance to your conclusion shows a high level of analysis.

This paragraph shows that **not** every aspect of Soviet industry changed and developed. Several things **stayed the same**. The living and working conditions of **Soviet workers** remained poor and the **purges** slowed industrial growth.

Finish your conclusion with a **Final Assessment**

You'll get a **good mark** if you:

1) Consider the **whole time period** in the question.

2) Show an understanding of how the situation **changed over time**.

You could try...

> Between 1928 and 1941 Soviet industry had changed and developed a lot, and by 1941 the USSR's industry was strong enough to survive the German invasion. However, the working conditions of many Soviets had hardly changed at all and the development of the consumer goods industry was slow.

Mentioning change and development shows that you're addressing the question.

You could **improve** this with more **detailed analysis**:

> In 1928 Stalin hoped to transform Soviet industry to compete with the USSR's rivals. He also hoped to shape the country so that the proletariat grew and the USSR became a fully industrialised country. By 1941 Soviet industry had grown enough for the USSR to be able to survive the German invasion. The country's economy was now driven by its heavy industry and the proletariat dominated the population. However, the economy hadn't changed or developed enough to improve the working life of the proletariat or provide them with consumer goods.

Here you've given some indication of the scale of the change and development.

This shows the examiner that you've made a balanced judgement.

Sample 'Why' Type Question

The 'why' type of question is the least common type of question you'll come across in the exam, but it's still important that you know how to answer them. So, here's a page that tells you all you need to know.

'Why' questions are about Causation

'Why' questions ask you to:

1) **Explain** the reasons a **historical event** or **situation** occurred in the way that it did.

2) Make a **judgement** as to what were the most **important** causes for the historical event or situation.

Occasionally you'll be asked to consider **two events**, e.g. 'Why was X able to defeat Y, but not Z?'

Highlight the Key Words in the question

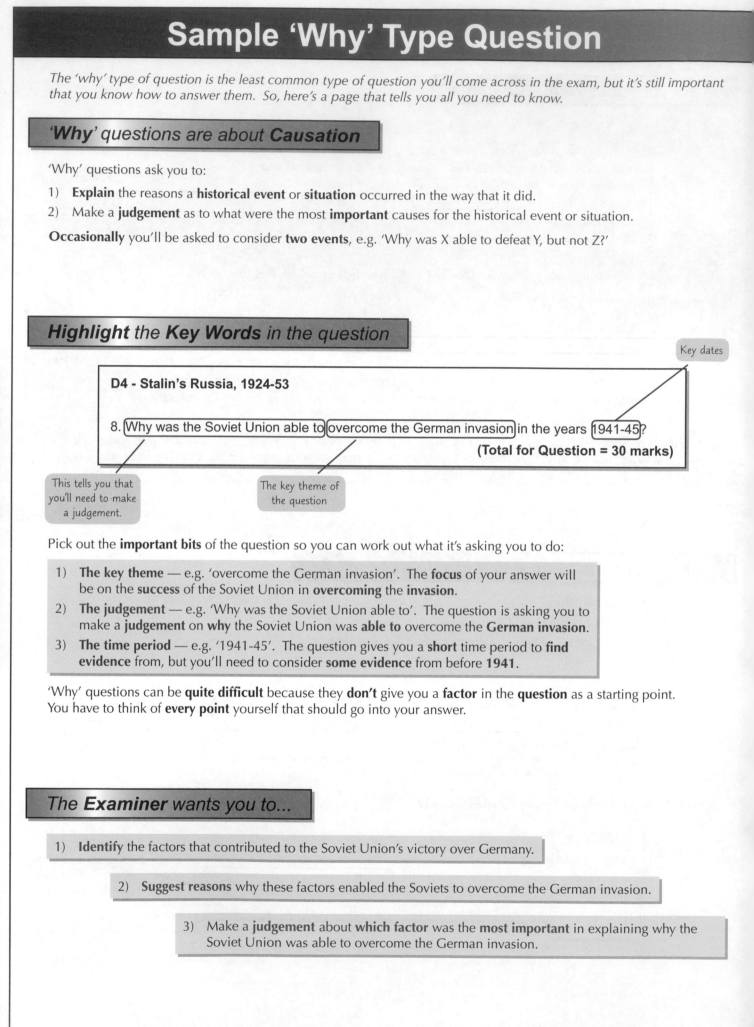

Key dates

D4 - Stalin's Russia, 1924-53

8. Why was the Soviet Union able to overcome the German invasion in the years 1941-45?

(Total for Question = 30 marks)

This tells you that you'll need to make a judgement.

The key theme of the question

Pick out the **important bits** of the question so you can work out what it's asking you to do:

1) **The key theme** — e.g. 'overcome the German invasion'. The **focus** of your answer will be on the **success** of the Soviet Union in **overcoming** the **invasion**.

2) **The judgement** — e.g. 'Why was the Soviet Union able to'. The question is asking you to make a **judgement** on **why** the Soviet Union was **able to** overcome the **German invasion**.

3) **The time period** — e.g. '1941-45'. The question gives you a **short** time period to **find evidence** from, but you'll need to consider **some evidence** from before **1941**.

'Why' questions can be **quite difficult** because they **don't** give you a **factor** in the **question** as a starting point. You have to think of **every point** yourself that should go into your answer.

The Examiner wants you to...

1) **Identify** the factors that contributed to the Soviet Union's victory over Germany.

2) **Suggest reasons** why these factors enabled the Soviets to overcome the German invasion.

3) Make a **judgement** about **which factor** was the **most important** in explaining why the Soviet Union was able to overcome the German invasion.

How to Select the Right Information

Here's the last set of mind-blowing pages which show you how to select the relevant information for the exam.

Select the Information that's Relevant to the Question

The question is asking you **why** the Soviet Union was **able to** overcome the German invasion, so you need to provide **evidence** that explains how the USSR was able to defeat the Nazis. You could start by looking at the Soviet Union's ability to **out-produce** the Germans and then look at what **policies** Stalin used to **raise** the **morale** of the Soviet people.

You'll find this info on Page 38...

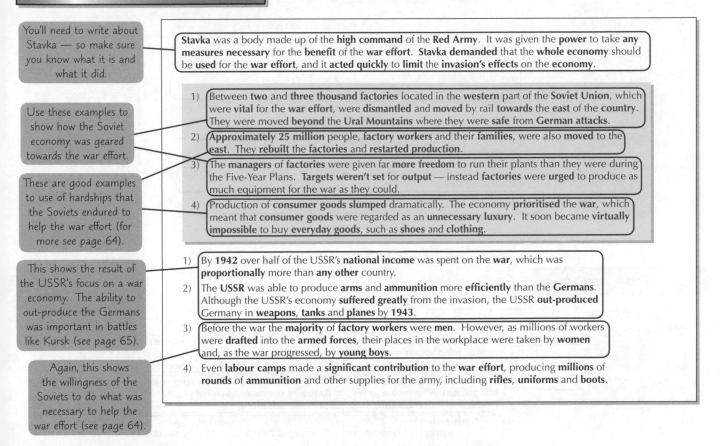

You'll need to write about Stavka — so make sure you know what it is and what it did.

> **Stavka** was a body made up of the **high command** of the **Red Army**. It was given the **power** to take **any measures necessary** for the **benefit** of the **war effort**. **Stavka demanded** that the **whole economy** should be **used** for the **war effort**, and it **acted quickly** to **limit** the **invasion's effects** on the **economy**.

Use these examples to show how the Soviet economy was geared towards the war effort.

1) Between **two** and **three thousand factories** located in the **western** part of the **Soviet Union**, which were **vital** for the **war effort**, were **dismantled** and **moved** by rail **towards** the **east** of the **country**. They were moved **beyond** the **Ural Mountains** where they were **safe** from **German attacks**.

2) **Approximately 25 million** people, **factory workers** and their **families**, were also **moved** to the **east**. They **rebuilt** the **factories** and **restarted production**.

These are good examples to use of hardships that the Soviets endured to help the war effort (for more see page 64).

3) The **managers** of **factories** were given far **more freedom** to run their plants than they were during the Five-Year Plans. **Targets weren't set** for **output** — instead **factories** were **urged** to produce as much equipment for the war as they could.

4) Production of **consumer goods slumped** dramatically. The economy **prioritised** the **war**, which meant that **consumer goods** were regarded as an **unnecessary luxury**. It soon became **virtually impossible** to buy **everyday goods**, such as **shoes** and **clothing**.

This shows the result of the USSR's focus on a war economy. The ability to out-produce the Germans was important in battles like Kursk (see page 65).

1) By **1942** over half of the USSR's **national income** was spent on the **war**, which was **proportionally** more than **any other** country.

2) The **USSR** was able to produce **arms** and **ammunition** more **efficiently** than the **Germans**. Although the USSR's economy **suffered greatly** from the invasion, the USSR **out-produced** Germany in **weapons**, **tanks** and **planes** by **1943**.

3) Before the war the **majority** of **factory workers** were **men**. However, as millions of workers were **drafted** into the **armed forces**, their places in the workplace were taken by **women** and, as the war progressed, by **young boys**.

Again, this shows the willingness of the Soviets to do what was necessary to help the war effort (see page 64).

4) Even **labour camps** made a **significant contribution** to the **war effort**, producing **millions** of **rounds** of **ammunition** and other supplies for the army, including **rifles**, **uniforms** and **boots**.

... and on Page 37

Stalin's reversal of his policy on religion raised the morale of the Soviet people. The morale of the people was important in helping to resist the invasion.

The **Communists** had **attacked religion** throughout their time in power, but Stalin **changed** this **policy** in **1943**.

1) In **1943** Stalin **reopened** many **churches** and **religious schools**.

2) He also **allowed** the **Russian Orthodox Church** to **elect** a **leader**, or **Patriarch**, for the **first time since** the **1917 October** Revolution.

3) In return the **Church agreed** to **support Stalin** and the **government**. It also **preached** in **favour** of the **'holy war'** against the invading **Germans**.

4) **Religion wasn't** truly **free** — it was **controlled** by **Stalin** and the **party** — but the **reopening** of **churches** gave the intended boost to Soviet **morale**.

You can give examples of Stalin's propaganda and mention how it raised the morale of the Soviet people.

1) **Stalin's propaganda emphasised** the **defence** of the "**Motherland**" by the USSR's "**brothers and sisters**".

2) **Stalin** was shown as a **wise leader** and **military strategist**, **working constantly** for the **defence** of the **Motherland**.

3) A **new national anthem** was **introduced** in **1944**, which **glorified** the **USSR**.

4) Shostakovich's *Leningrad Symphony* (see page 32), which was **composed** in the **besieged city**, was **broadcast across** the **USSR**.

How to Select the Right Information

You should also look at the *Strength* of *Soviet Resistance*

One of the **most important** reasons why the Soviets were able to overcome the German invasion was the **strength** of the **Soviet resistance** — of both the **Red Army** and the **Soviet people**.

You'll find this info on *Page 35*...

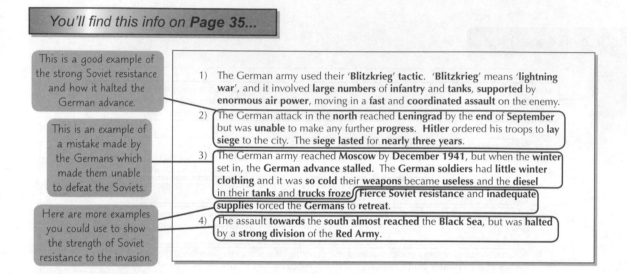

This is a good example of the strong Soviet resistance and how it halted the German advance.

1) The German army used their 'Blitzkrieg' tactic. 'Blitzkrieg' means 'lightning war', and it involved large numbers of infantry and tanks, supported by enormous air power, moving in a fast and coordinated assault on the enemy.

This is an example of a mistake made by the Germans which made them unable to defeat the Soviets.

2) The German attack in the north reached Leningrad by the end of September but was unable to make any further progress. Hitler ordered his troops to lay siege to the city. The siege lasted for nearly three years.

3) The German army reached Moscow by December 1941, but when the winter set in, the German advance stalled. The German soldiers had little winter clothing and it was so cold their weapons became useless and the diesel in their tanks and trucks froze. Fierce Soviet resistance and inadequate supplies forced the Germans to retreat.

Here are more examples you could use to show the strength of Soviet resistance to the invasion.

4) The assault towards the south almost reached the Black Sea, but was halted by a strong division of the Red Army.

... and on *Page 36*...

You can mention how Stalin's leadership strengthened the Soviet resistance.

1) After disappearing from public view in the early days of the war, Stalin returned to provide effective leadership. Stalin stayed in Moscow, even though it seemed the city would fall to the Germans, and his presence boosted the morale of the Soviet soldiers.

You could write a little bit about some of the tactics used by the Soviets to defeat the Germans.

2) The Soviets used a 'scorched earth' policy as they retreated — sabotaging roads and bridges, destroying food supplies and damaging communication lines — making it harder for the German army to get supplies as it advanced.

3) The Nazis' racism hurt Germany's war effort. Many Soviets didn't like Stalin and were willing to support the Germans, but they changed their minds when the Germans treated the people under their control brutally.

This was an important mistake by the Nazis that you can mention in your essay. It ended up strengthening the Soviet resistance.

4) Rumours of atrocities spread to the rest of the USSR, and most Soviets realised that they had to be prepared to fight to the death in what Stalin called the 'Great Patriotic War'.

... and on *Page 37*

Here are some more examples of hardships endured by the Soviets in their effort to resist the German invasion.

1) Despite the best efforts of the farmers, food was in desperately short supply in the towns.

2) Food was rationed according to the amount of work that was done. Only those who worked were given a ration card — those who couldn't work were left to fend for themselves.

3) Many people had to survive on less than the official daily ration and millions starved to death.

4) Workers were expected to work seven days a week without holidays.

5) Most homes were without electricity for most of the war.

How to Select the Right Information

Find any other **Relevant** information

You should look for some **external factors** that explain how the **USSR** was able to **overcome** the **German invasion** — **Lend-Lease** is a good example to look at. You could also look at the **most important battles** between the USSR and Germany and see **why** the **Soviet Union** was able to **emerge victorious**.

You'll find this info on **Page 39**...

These are good examples of things that Lend-Lease provided which you can mention in your essays.

1) **Very little** reached the **USSR** from the West **until 1943**. Compared to what the USSR produced, **Western support** was **relatively small**, but it was **vital** in **certain areas**.
2) **Radio equipment** sent to the USSR improved the Red Army's battlefield communications. It meant that **troops** could be **directed rapidly** and **efficiently**.
3) **Lend-Lease** provided some of the **vital** raw materials that were in **short supply** (e.g. **aluminium**, **copper** and **coal**) after the USSR's loss of the **Donbass region**.
4) **Specialists** were sent to the **USSR**, and Soviet technicians visited the West to **study** techniques to **improve** the **quality** of **armaments** and **increase production**.
5) **Food production** in the USSR had **slumped** since **Germany** seized the **grain fields** of Ukraine. **Lend-Lease** supplied millions of **tons** of **food**, including **vast quantities** of Spam. **Khrushchev**, the leader who **succeeded Stalin**, claimed **Spam** was **essential** to the **Red Army's victory**.

These are the most important things that Lend-Lease provided and they contributed to the Soviet victory.

You could balance a point about Lend-Lease by saying that the USSR was able to produce most of what it needed without US assistance.

1) The **USSR's rail network** was in a **poor condition** in **1942**. **Lend-Lease** helped to **ease** this **problem** with **large shipments** of **track**, **engines** and **wagons** to transport both **men** and **supplies**. As a result, **millions of troops** could be **moved quickly** to **different parts** of the **Eastern Front**.
2) The **USA** supplied the **USSR** with **approximately 375 000 trucks** and **50 000 jeeps**. These were **very important** in **supplying frontline troops** — they **allowed** the **Red Army** to **move quickly** against the **Germans without losing touch** with their **supply lines**.
3) The **USSR produced most** of its **own tanks** and **aircraft** — it didn't need much of these from the **West**. For example, when it was first introduced, the **Soviet T-34** tank was **more effective** than **most tanks built** in the **West**.

... and on **Page 36**

Here is another example of the strength of the Soviet resistance. Many citizens were prepared to fight to the death.

1) In **1942 Hitler** ordered an **attack** on **Stalingrad**. His aim was to seize the city to allow the **German army** to push **south** and **capture** the **oil fields** of the **Caucasus region**.
2) Within a **few months** the **fighting** had reached the **city's suburbs**. Stalin ordered **every able-bodied citizen** to be supplied with a **rifle** so that they could **defend** the **city**.
3) By **November**, German troops had **entered** the **city** and **weeks** of **fierce house-to-house fighting** followed. The Germans **almost captured** the **whole city** before the tide turned.
4) **Soviet forces** under **Marshal Zhukov** began a **counter-attack** outside of the city, **cutting off** the **German supply lines**. They **trapped** most of the German army **inside** the **city**.

Stalingrad was a crucial victory for the Soviets and gave them the belief that they could overcome the invasion.

5) **Surrounded** and **starving**, the German soldiers eventually **surrendered** on **2nd February 1943**. **90 000 German soldiers** were **taken prisoner**.
6) The **victory** at **Stalingrad raised** the **morale** of the **Red Army** and **humiliated** the **Germans**.

The Soviets were able to out-produce the Germans in military equipment (see page 63). This gave them an important advantage at battles like Kursk.

1) In **1943**, the **Germans** deployed around **700 000 men** at **Kursk**, **supported** by roughly **2700 tanks**. The **Red Army** had **approximately 1.3 million men** at the battle, with up to **3300 tanks**.
2) After the initial German attack, the **Soviets** mounted a powerful **counter-attack** which **smashed** the **German line**. The **Germans** were **forced** to **retreat**.
3) Kursk was the **largest tank battle** of the war and it was a more **decisive victory** than Stalingrad. There were **massive losses** on **both sides**, but the **German army** in the **east** had been **broken**.

How to Plan Your Answer

This page will help you plan for 'why' type questions, like the one on page 62.

Use a **Plan** to **Structure** your **Argument**

Here's the question again:

> Why was the Soviet Union able to overcome the German invasion in the years 1941-45?

Once you've got your **evidence** you're going to have to **organise** it into an essay.
A plan will help you do this. You shouldn't spend more than **5 minutes**, so **don't** waste time.
Your plan could include:

1) **4-5 factors** which the USSR controlled that helped them to overcome the **German invasion**.

2) **2-3 external factors** which helped the USSR overcome the **German invasion**.

3) Some notes on your **conclusion**.

Then you can:

1) Think of all the different **reasons/causes/factors** which will help you **answer the question**.

2) You need to decide how best to **organise** these reasons/causes/factors to answer the question. You could put them in order of **importance** or separate them into **internal** and **external** factors. For questions that ask about a longer time period, you could organise your answer **chronologically**, or organise it into **long-term**, **short-term** and **immediate** causes or factors.

3) However you organise your points, you must put together an **answer to the question**. **Analyse** the key points and come to a **judgement** — don't just write a list or tell the story.

4) Select **relevant supporting material** for each point.

Here's an **Example Plan**

Your plan probably won't be as big as this. We've written it in full so it's easier to follow.

1. Economic and Industrial Factors in the USSR's victory.
- Stavka organised the war effort — whole economy focused on the war.
- Soviet industry was moved east of the Urals, away from German attacks.
- USSR managed to out-produce Germany in military equipment — important in key battles.

2. Military factors in the USSR's victory.
- 1941 was disastrous for the Soviets — but Soviet resistance was strong. Halted German advance in 1941 and the major cities survived long sieges.
- Soviet civilians kept up resistance through German attacks.
- 'Scorched earth' policy slowed the German advance.
- Red Army won crucial battles at Stalingrad and Kursk.

Overcoming the German invasion

3. Political Factors in the USSR's victory.
- Stalin showed strong leadership from Moscow.
- Stalin stopped persecution of religion — boosted morale.
- Soviet propaganda strengthened resolve of the people.

5. Conclusion
- External factors were important in the Soviet Union's victory, especially the German mistakes.
- However, the most important factor was the Soviet resistance to the initial German attack. Had cities like Leningrad, Moscow and Stalingrad fallen then the war would have been over.
- Soviet resistance gave time for the USSR to produce enough tanks, aircraft and weapons to defeat the Germans.

4. External factors contributing to Soviet victory.
- German mistakes — like committing atrocities against the Soviet people. Strengthened their resolve to fight to the death.
- Lend-Lease contributed to the Soviet war effort.
- Cold weather caused major problems for the German army.

Worked Answer

Ahh... we're almost finished, but before I go, here are some more pages that will help you to improve your essays.

A good *Introduction* will *Guide* your essay

You could start with:

> There were many reasons why the Soviet Union was able to overcome the German invasion during the years 1941-45. Despite a bad start, the USSR was able to organise both military and civilian resistance on a massive scale. After the Battle of Kursk in 1943 the Germans began to retreat and they were eventually defeated in 1945.

This shows that you're focusing on the question.

Here you've given reasons why the USSR was successful.

This intro is **okay** because it:

1) **Focuses** on the **question**.

2) Mentions some important **dates**.

3) Suggests **some reasons** that explain why the Soviet Union **overcame** the **Germans**.

However, it's a bit **vague**. 'Why' questions are more difficult because you need to think of all the **different reasons yourself** — a **better** introduction would include more **detail**, like this:

> The USSR was able to overcome the German invasion through the combination of many key factors — it overtook Germany in the production of weapons thanks to Stavka, its civillians and army stood up and halted Germany's attack in 1941, and its military won key battles like Kursk and Stalingrad. Furthermore, the USSR was aided by external factors like the Lend-Lease scheme, and important mistakes made by their German enemies.

Here you've shown that external factors contributed to the USSR's victory.

You could start by looking at how Soviets *Out-produced* the Nazis

You could begin with:

> One of the main reasons for the Soviet victory was their ability to outproduce the Nazis. The Soviets set up a central command centre, or Stavka. Stavka coordinated the role of the military, the economy and the civilian population in the war with Germany. For example, Soviet industry was rebuilt and relocated east of the Ural Mountains and the production of military equipment increased.

Good use of historical term.

1) These sentences **describe** how the **Soviet command structure** worked, but they **don't** explain **why** this enabled the Soviets to overcome the Germans.

2) To **improve** this you should give some **reasons** to **explain** why this enabled the Soviets to be successful:

> Stavka was created to help the USSR to coordinate its war effort against the Germans. Stavka tried to ensure that the military, industry and the civilian population all worked together to overcome the Germans. From 1942 Soviet industry was relocated and rebuilt to the east of the Ural Mountains so that it was beyond the reach of German forces. Soviet industry was also concentrated on producing military equipment. In 1943 the Soviets had more tanks than the Germans at the Battle of Kursk and were able to defeat them.

This shows why relocating industry was important.

This shows that the Soviet Union's ability to out-produce the Germans in military equipment contributed to their success in battle.

Worked Answer

You could look at how the Soviets were determined to **Win** at **All Costs**

You could start with:

> Soviet civilians put up fierce resistance to the German invasion. The cities of Leningrad and Stalingrad were both besieged for many months. The civilians inside were strong enough to hold out and not surrender.

This introduces the idea that the **Soviet civilians** fought against the German invasion, but it **doesn't** explain why this **enabled** the **Soviet Union** to **succeed**.

This makes it clear that your point is relevant to the question.

This links the strength of the Soviet civilian resistance to the USSR's ability to out-produce the Germans.

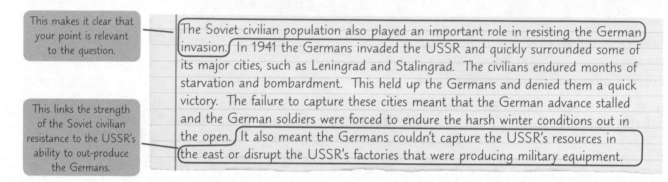

The Soviet civilian population also played an important role in resisting the German invasion. In 1941 the Germans invaded the USSR and quickly surrounded some of its major cities, such as Leningrad and Stalingrad. The civilians endured months of starvation and bombardment. This held up the Germans and denied them a quick victory. The failure to capture these cities meant that the German advance stalled and the German soldiers were forced to endure the harsh winter conditions out in the open. It also meant the Germans couldn't capture the USSR's resources in the east or disrupt the USSR's factories that were producing military equipment.

You now need to look at how **External Factors** helped the Soviet Union

The USSR's allies provided help to their war effort and you need to explain **how** this contributed to the USSR's **success**.

You could start with:

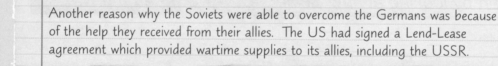

> Another reason why the Soviets were able to overcome the Germans was because of the help they received from their allies. The US had signed a Lend-Lease agreement which provided wartime supplies to its allies, including the USSR.

This paragraph introduces another **relevant** factor that helps to **explain** Soviet **success** in overcoming the **Germans**, but you could **improve** it by:
1) Stating the **importance** of the **factor**.
2) **Explaining** how it helped the Soviets overcome the Germans.

You could write...

These are good examples of what Lend-Lease provided.

The help that the USSR received from its allies contributed to the defeat of the Germans. The US extended Lend-Lease to provide supplies such as radio communications equipment and food to the Soviets. Above all, Lend-Lease provided many of the trains, jeeps and trucks used by the Soviets. The help provided by the US didn't directly win any victories for the Soviets in battle, but it gave an important boost to their war effort and allowed Soviet industry to focus on producing tanks and weapons.

Worked Answer

Try to **Link** some points together

You could write:

> This is an external factor that helped the Soviet Union overcome the German invasion.

> The Germans also made some big mistakes that contributed to the USSR's victory. Many Soviets hated Stalin, and when the Germans invaded they welcomed them. However, the Nazis' racism meant that the Germans treated Soviet civilians badly and rumours of atrocities caused any goodwill towards the Germans to disappear.

This paragraph is **fine** and it introduces a good point — that the Germans contributed to their own defeat. However, it would be **better** if you could **continue** the point by **linking** it to **another factor**:

> Here you've indicated how important you think the factor is.

> The Germans' poor treatment of Soviet citizens convinced many Soviets that they were in a fight to the death. This made them even more determined to resist the Nazi invasion and it gave them extra resolve, even when they were faced with great hardship, such as during the siege of Leningrad and at the Battle of Stalingrad. This was a major factor in the Soviet Union's victory over Germany.

> You've linked your original point about an external factor to a point about resolve of the Soviet people.

Decide which points are the **Most Important** for your **Conclusion**

You could begin by writing...

> In conclusion, the Soviets were able to overcome the German invasion due to a combination of a strong government-organised resistance and some help from external factors, in particular the Germans' poor treatment of the Soviet people and the help received from the USSR's allies.

This conclusion is **okay**, because it picks out several different **reasons** to explain why the Soviet Union was able to **overcome** the **Germans**, however it doesn't provide enough detail and it doesn't give a clear judgement.

You could write about how the Soviets **themselves** were able to **overcome** the **Germans**:

> The resolve of the Soviet citizens was by far the most important reason for the defeat of the Germans. The citizens of the USSR showed great resolve in the face of terrible hardships and this enabled the Soviets to halt the German advance. The other main factor was Stavka's successful organising of the war effort to maximise the USSR's ability to out-produce Germany in military equipment. This also contributed significantly to the USSR's defeat of Germany.

> Here you've made a judgement that you think this was the most important factor.

This is good because you've made a **judgement** as to which factor you think was the **most important**, but you can make this **better** by comparing it to other factors to **justify** your **choice**:

> The resolve of the Soviet citizens was by far the most important reason why the Soviet Union was able to overcome the Germans. The Germans themselves contributed to this strong resistance by treating Soviet citizens badly and convincing them that they were in a fight to the death. Other factors played an important role in the Soviet victory. For example, Lend-Lease provided invaluable support to the Soviet war effort, and the organisation of Stavka was crucial in the eventual defeat of the Germans. But if the Soviet people had crumbled before the USSR could strike back then the Germans would have won very quickly.

> This is a good argument to support your judgement.

It **doesn't** matter what way you write your conclusion, but make a **judgement** on which **reasons** you think were the **most important** in **explaining** why the Soviets were **able to overcome** the **German invasion** in the years 1941-45.

Index